Holy Spirit
YOUR HELPER

FAITH A. OYEDEPO

HOLY SPIRIT: YOUR HELPER
Copyright © 2019 by:
Faith A. Oyedepo
ISBN 978-2480-51-7

Published in Nigeria by:
DOMINION PUBLISHING HOUSE

For further information or permission, address:

DOMINION PUBLISHING HOUSE
Km 10, Idiroko Road, Canaanland, Ota, Nigeria.
Tel: +234 816 406 0777, +234 909 151 4022

Or visit our website: ***www.dphprints.com***

Connect with Faith Oyedepo

🄵 Faith Abiola Oyedepo   🐦 faithoyedepo

📷 @officialfaithoyedepo   🌐 www.faithoyedepo.org

All Scripture quotations are from the King James Version of the Bible, except otherwise stated.

CONTENTS

Introduction

For the kingdom of God is not in word, but in power.

1 Corinthians 4:20

From the happenings around the world, various crimes, tales of wars, scarcity and wickedness, it is evident that we are in the last days. The Bible clearly states, ***This know also, that in the last days perilous times shall come*** (2 Timothy 3:1). However, the last days are also identified as the days of the reign of the church of God. Believers will clearly exercise dominion in the world, but that dominion can only be possible via access to a higher power.

Clearly, every child of God is ordained to reign on the earth (Revelation 5:10), but you cannot reign without the power of the Holy Spirit. Your greatness is determined by the level of power you have access to. Please understand that the power I am referring to in this book is not ordinary. It is neither the man-made show of authority nor is it fetish; it is the power of the Holy Spirit.

Life without the Holy Spirit is an adventure in futility and will only result in unending frustration. Not until recently, the church didn't pay much attention to the baptism and infilling of the Holy Spirit, and so was limited in effect and manifestations. However, when the move of the Spirit of God came upon the church, power sprung forth and diverse manifestations of signs and wonders became the order of the day.

However, even with diverse manifestations of the Holy Spirit in the church today, the power from on high is still being underutilised. If the church as a whole has not yet arrived in actualising the full access to the power of the Holy Spirit, it means that neither have many of us; hence, the need for this book.

The quality of your walk with God can be far better than it is today; you can gain deeper access to the things of God beyond your imagination. However, it lies in your access to empowerment and re-empowerment by the power of the Holy Spirit. It is written,

> **And, behold, I send the promise of my Father upon you: but tarry ye in the city of Jerusalem, until ye be endued with power from on high.**
>
> *Luke 24:49*

As you read this book with an open heart, I trust that God will launch you into a higher realm of the many-sided dimensions of the power of the Holy Spirit and enable you to maximally tap into what that power offers for a most exciting and fulfilling Christian adventure in life.

To fully accomplish your purpose on earth, the oppositions notwithstanding, you need the power of the Holy Spirit in a growing dimension, and the more empowered you are, the greater your exploits in life.

The good news is this: God's power is available and accessible to all, but it can only be received on demand. Join me as we explore and experience a fresh baptism of the power of the Holy Spirit together!

Understanding The Power Of The Holy Spirit

For the kingdom of God is not in word, but in power.

1 Corinthians 4:20

We live in a world that is power-conscious and dominion-driven. The crave for power, amply characterised by the various happenings around the world today, is the order of the day. Stronger nations are constantly aspiring to take over supposedly weaker nations and everyone seems to want to outdo the other in this chase for dominion.

However, dominion is a function of power (Psalm 66:3) and power is an essential part of our everyday life. From scriptures, we understand that the more 'powerful' we become, the sweeter and more sweatless our adventure in life would be. This is because power puts us in command and ahead of oppositions any day and at any time.

What Is Power?

Power, according to *the Free Dictionary*, is the ability or capacity to perform or act effectively. It is also a specific capacity, strength or force exerted or capable of being exerted. It represents might and the ability or official capacity to exercise control.

To make the most of our lives and destinies, we need power to act effectively in our given task. From the above definition, we also see the word 'control' and that connotes the ability to direct or manage a specific assignment.

Also, according to *Merriam-Webster Dictionary*, power is the ability to act or produce an effect; legal or official authority, capacity, or right; a possession of control, or influence over others.

Biblical Definition of Power

Power, from the biblical perspective, can be referred to as **delegated authority.** This means the power conferred on a person to give orders and to make others obey. We must understand that authority is neither inborn nor inherited; rather, it is conferred on an individual.

During the latter part of Jesus earthly ministry, He called His disciples and sent them forth giving them power, which connotes delegated authority, over unclean spirits. It is written,

And he called unto him the twelve, and began to send them forth by two and two; and gave them power over unclean spirits.

Mark 6:7

This means that wherever they went, no devil was permitted to torment them because they had delegated authority over the works of darkness. The Bible says,

Behold, I give unto you power to tread on serpents and scorpions, and over all the power of the enemy: and nothing shall by any means hurt you.

Luke 10:19

The essence of this authority is for you to subdue the enemy. Life in itself is full of oppositions. My husband, Dr. David Oyedepo said, 'Life is warfare and not a funfair'. Actually, we fight oppositions daily and at all levels of life. That is why it is important to be endued with power.

Jesus, before His ascension, told His disciples, *And, behold, I send the promise of my Father upon you: but tarry ye in the city of Jerusalem, until ye be endued with power (delegated authority) from on high* (Luke 24:49, Emphasis mine).

Please understand: The devil goes around seeking whom he may devour (1 Peter 5:8), but he can only devour those who are powerless and helpless. So, for us to make the most of our journey in life and not be rendered helpless, we need power over the forces that may want to stand in the way.

Power also connotes **strength,** the strength of God in the affairs of men. Putting the biblical account of how God led the Israelites out of Egypt into perspective, we saw the power of God at work. Referring to Pharaoh, God said,

> *And in very deed for this cause have I raised thee up, for to shew in thee my power; and that my name may be declared throughout all the earth.*
>
> Exodus 9:16

'Power' in the above scripture refers to engaging God's strength in rescuing Israel from bondage. That was why after Moses and the people crossed the red sea, they said,

> *Thy right hand, O LORD, is become glorious in power: thy right hand, O LORD, hath dashed in pieces the enemy.*
>
> Exodus 15:6

In another account, while Nehemiah prayed for favour to rebuild the walls of Jerusalem, he said, *Now these are thy servants and thy people, whom thou hast redeemed by thy great power, and by thy strong hand* (Nehemiah 1:10).

Power may also mean a man's physical strength in accomplishing a task. That is why when a person does something that seems extraordinary, you hear statements like 'he or she is very powerful'. The 'power' there connotes that the person is endowed with the much needed strength to accomplish that task.

Power can also be seen as the **anointing** of the Holy Spirit. It was said of Jesus that He returned in the power of the Holy Spirit (Luke 4:14); He came in the anointing of the Holy Ghost. This anointing enabled Him to accomplish great exploits in ministry (Isaiah 61:1).

Power is **dominion** over the forces of hell and the challenges of life. This means authority to rule; and you will agree with me that you cannot have the authority to rule, if power has not been conferred on you. As it is written,

> *And he that overcometh, and keepeth my works unto the end, to him will I give power over the nations.*
>
> Revelation 2:26

Some years ago, my husband, Dr. David Oyedepo, visited the nation of Liberia for a crusade. Prior to his arrival, an occultic woman known as the queen of Sheba lodged in the same hotel where he lodged. Immediately he stepped into that hotel, I believe hell knew that a higher power had arrived. That night, the so-called queen of Sheba who was welcomed into that town with so much pomp and pageantry became restless and instantly left the country unceremoniously! Even the national newspaper of that country published an article on her unusual departure and also acknowledged the fact that a higher power had come into the nation.

The truth is: Even though the Bible records that God has given us dominion over everything on the earth, you cannot have dominion without power. It is written,

> **And God said, Let us make man in our image, after our likeness: and let them have dominion over the fish of the sea, and over the fowl of the air, and over the cattle, and over all the earth, and over every creeping thing that creepeth upon the earth.**
>
> *Genesis 1:26*

Therefore, to truly walk in the actualisation of this dominion, you need not just power, but adequate power!

Types of Power

Basically, there are two different types of power. There is the divine or God's power, which is constructive in nature, and the power of darkness, which is always destructive. God's power is however, supreme to all other powers.

Constructive Power

The word 'constructive' means having a useful purpose. The purpose of this type of power is to build or edify a person, group or an organisation. God is the only source of constructive power. For instance, we are saved through Christ by the power of God. Salvation is the ultimate gift of God to man. Before then, man was lost and without hope (Ephesians 2:12). When Jesus was crucified on the cross, God's power raised Him up and that brought salvation to man. The Word of God says,

> *For though he was crucified through weakness, yet he liveth by the power of God. For we also are weak in him, but we shall live with him by the power of God toward you.*
>
> *2 Corinthians 13:4*

God's power did not only bring salvation to man, it also brought peace, joy and increase to the lives of all that believe.

Moses and all the hosts of Israel were brought out of captivity by the power of God (Exodus 14:30; Jeremiah 32:21).

Moreover, Jesus being anointed of the Holy Ghost and with power went about doing good and healing all that were oppressed of the devil (Acts 10:38). Jesus could do such mighty works because the power of God backed Him up. It was through the power of God that He was able to heal the sick, raise the dead and perform miracles. Remember He said,

> *I can of mine own self do nothing...*
>
> *John 5:30*

Paul and Silas were supernaturally released from captivity by the power of God through the mystery of praise (Acts 16:25-26). So, God's power can penetrate any circumstance, at any time, to perform what God has ordained.

However, it is clear from scriptures that God's power is not only constructive, but can also be positively destructive. It can destroy the work and planting of the devil in our lives to give us a more victorious life. It is written,

> **Say unto God, How terrible art thou in thy works! through the greatness of thy power shall thine enemies submit themselves unto thee.**
>
> *Psalm 66:3*

The truth is: Your enemies will not submit themselves to you without power. The world is constantly ruled by power and the lesser power must always bow to the stronger. Remember, whatever is from above is above all (John 3:31). God's power, which is from above, is the ultimate power and that is why believers need to always crave it. The deeper you are in God, the more powerful you will be and the more terrifying you become to the kingdom of darkness. This is because the devil is always afraid of those who are divinely empowered.

Destructive Power

Satanic power is strictly destructive in nature (Colossians 1:13). The purpose of this is to oppose all the good works of God for mankind. From the beginning, the devil has been the author of destruction. When he saw the peace, serenity and abundance Adam and Eve had in the Garden of Eden, he came with his deceit, which is his major tool of destruction, to displace man from the original plan God had for him. As it is written,

> *The thief cometh not, but for to steal, and to kill, and to destroy: I am come that they might have life, and that they might have it more abundantly*
> *John 10:10*

Clearly, the devil has no good intentions for anyone. There is nothing he gives that does not destroy or leave the recipient miserable. He is the father of all lies and tricks; as such, he has nothing good to offer. Therefore, we must beware of his devices, so we don't fall into his traps (2 Corinthians 2:11).

What is this Power from on High?

It is important to understand that the power from on high, as we have established, is not physical or intellectual, but divine. It is written,

> *...The <u>Holy Ghost</u> shall come upon thee, and <u>the power of the Highest</u> shall overshadow thee...*
> *Luke 1:35 (Emphasis mine)*

Clearly, the Holy Spirit is the power from on high!

Jesus said,

> *But ye shall receive <u>power</u>, after that the <u>Holy Ghost</u>*
> *is come upon you...*
>
> *Acts 1:8 (Emphasis mine)*

The Holy Spirit is the power of God on the earth for the benefit of the end-time believers. God knew that man would require divine intervention to be able to successfully journey through this wicked and perverse world; so, He made provision for the Holy Spirit, who is the custodian of God's power, to strengthen us to walk in God's glorious plan.

Notably, even Jesus, our perfect example, had to be endued with the Holy Spirit and power for ministry. After He received the power from on high, the Bible records that His fame went through all the regions (Luke 4:14).

The Holy Spirit is our ever-available and dependable helper. He is the power that never fails. However, when you are baptised with the Holy Spirit, with the evidence of speaking in tongues, the tongues that you speak is the proof, indication and sign that the deposit of the power from on high is available and within your reach for triumphant living.

At salvation, the seed of God's power is deposited inside you. The fruits of this seed include triumph, victory, dominion, etc. The Bible records,

How God anointed Jesus of Nazareth with the Holy

Ghost and with power: who went about doing good,
and healing all that were oppressed of the devil; for
God was with him.

Acts 10:38

The power of the Holy Spirit supernaturally delivers from every oppression of the enemy (Luke 5:17). This power is not physical, emotional or political; it cannot be bought with money or any material possession. Remember, when Simon in Acts 8 saw the effect of the power of God through the Holy Spirit in the lives of the Apostles, he offered to buy it with money for his selfish aim. Then Peter told him,

...Thy money perish with thee, because thou hast
thought that the gift of God may be purchased with
money.

Acts 8:20

Clearly, the power from on high supersedes all other powers and it is the most valuable asset in our Christian Journey. Therefore, it is wisdom to go for it. May you have an unforgettable encounter with the power of the Holy Spirit as you go through this book, in Jesus name!

Exploring The Dimensions Of The Holy Spirit

Now unto him that is able to do exceeding abundantly above all that we ask or think, according to the power that worketh in us.

Ephesians 3:20

There is a power at work in every believer; it is the power of God – the power from on high; the power of the Holy Spirit. God's power is great; it is unfathomable. Every enemy bows to the greatness of God's power and you subdue every opposition cheaply by the power of the Holy Spirit. The Bible says,

Say unto God, How terrible art thou in thy works! through the greatness of thy power shall thine enemies submit themselves unto thee.

Psalm 66:3

God's power is manifested through the Holy Spirit.

He is the custodian of God's power on the earth. It is the Holy Spirit that makes manifest the efficacy of the power from on high. Without Him, power will be inaccessible to the believer. It is written,

> *But ye shall receive power, after that the Holy Ghost is come upon you: and ye shall be witnesses unto me both in Jerusalem, and in all Judaea, and in Samaria, and unto the uttermost part of the earth.*
> *Acts 1:8*

However, there are dimensions of this power from on high as clearly enumerated in scriptures and some of them shall be briefly examined in this chapter.

The Power at Salvation

This power makes you confess Jesus as your personal Lord and Saviour. No man has the power to convict or draw any soul to Christ, except God. At salvation, it is the power of God through the Holy Spirit that enables man to confess Jesus Christ as Lord and Saviour. Scripture says,

> *...No man can say that Jesus is the Lord, but by the Holy Ghost.*
> *1 Corinthians 12:3*

At salvation, by the enabling of the Holy Spirit, you are empowered to become a son of God. The Bible says,

> *But as many as received him, to them gave he power to become the sons of God, even to them that*

believe on his name.

John 1:12

Also, it is written,

> *For I am not ashamed of the gospel of Christ: for it is the power of God unto salvation to every one that believeth; to the Jew first, and also to the Greek.*

Romans 1:16

At salvation, it is the power of the Holy Spirit in the Word of God that convicts you to repent of your sins and be born again. When you listen to God's Word, He enables you through the Holy Spirit to believe in Jesus, who is the Way, the Truth and the Life (John 14:6). It is your belief in Jesus that makes you confess Him as Lord.

What is Salvation?

Salvation is an experience of new birth. It means to be born again. It is the regeneration of one's spirit-man from the earthly nature of sin to the heavenly, which is characterised by righteousness. It is the passport or major prerequisite for receiving the power from on high.

But, how can one become born again?

- **Acknowledge that you are a sinner:** The first step to salvation is to accept that you are a sinner in dire need of a way of escape. The Bible says that all have sinned and fallen short of God's glory (Romans 3:23). The Bible says,

If we say that we have no sin, we deceive ourselves, and the truth is not in us.

1 John 1:8

- **Repent and consciously ask God for forgiveness:** It is not enough to acknowledge your sins; you must proceed to repentance and consciously ask God for forgiveness. This means confessing every fault to God with a genuine heart of repentance. Even though it is impossible to remember every sin you might have committed, just confess the ones you can remember and ask Him to forgive you. It is written,

Then Peter said unto them, Repent, and be baptized every one of you in the name of Jesus Christ for the remission of sins, and ye shall receive the gift of the Holy Ghost.

Acts 2:38

- **Believe and confess Jesus as your Saviour:** Without believing in God's power to forgive you your sins, it is impossible to become a beneficiary of His power at salvation. It is your faith in the power of Jesus to forgive and cleanse you of your sins that gives you the confidence that you are now born again and can walk in the reality of new birth. It is written,

For with the heart man believeth unto righteousness; and with the mouth confession is made unto salvation.

Romans 10:10

When you confess Jesus Christ as your Saviour and Lord, you are then born again and become a beneficiary of the power at salvation. My question to you at this point is: Have you consciously accepted Jesus Christ as your personal Saviour and Lord? Are you born again, saved and a child of God? Until this is done, you cannot receive the power from on high.

As a teenager, I accepted Jesus Christ as my Lord and personal Saviour. My life was transformed and has never been the same again. I thank God I took that decision! If you want to be born again, please go to the end of this book now and say the prayer of salvation in faith.

Power at Holy Ghost Baptism

This represents the infilling of the Holy Ghost and this infilling comes with power. Therefore, when you consciously ask God and you are baptised with the Holy Spirit, you receive power with which you can quench all the fiery darts of the enemy, walk in righteousness and fulfil God's glorious plan for your life. It is written,

> *But ye shall receive power, after that the Holy Ghost is come upon you...*
>
> *Acts 1:8*

Understand that speaking in tongues is the evidence of your being filled with the Holy Ghost. You cannot claim to be filled with the power at Holy Ghost baptism without the clear evidence of speaking in tongues.

Tongues is the heavenly language that identifies you as a carrier of the indwelling power of the Holy Spirit. As it is written,

> *And these signs shall follow them that believe; In my name shall they cast out devils; they shall speak with <u>new tongues</u>.*
>
> *Mark 16:17 (Emphasis mine)*

When the disciples were filled with the Holy Spirit in the upper room, they were all heard speaking in other tongues as proof that they were filled. The Bible records,

> *And they were all filled with the Holy Ghost, and began to speak with <u>other tongues</u>, as the Spirit gave them utterance.*
>
> *Acts 2:4 (Emphasis mine)*

However, you cannot receive the power of the Holy Ghost without first receiving the power at salvation. Power at salvation necessarily precedes the baptism of the Holy Ghost. That is, the power of the Holy Spirit is only given to you after you have received power to become a son of God.

For instance, Saul, who later became Paul, had an encounter with Jesus on his way to Damascus, before he was baptised with the Holy Ghost after Ananias prayed for him (Acts 9:1-17). The people of Samaria also received salvation when Philip witnessed the Word to them. Thereafter, Peter and John were sent to them so they could be baptised in the Holy Ghost. Scripture says,

Now when the apostles which were at Jerusalem heard that Samaria had received the word of God, they sent unto them Peter and John:

Who, when they were come down, prayed for them, that they might receive the Holy Ghost:

Then laid they their hands on them, and they received the Holy Ghost.

Acts 8:14-15, 17

Cornelius and his household were baptised in the Holy Ghost after they believed the Word of God spoken to them by Peter. As it is written,

While Peter yet spake these words, the Holy Ghost fell on all them which heard the word.

Acts 10:44

The disciples in Ephesus, who Paul met on the way, were only baptised in water. This means that they were born again, but had not received or heard of the baptism of the Holy Spirit. So, they were filled with the Holy Spirit when Paul prayed for them, after they had been saved (Acts 19:1-7).

Please understand: Holy Ghost baptism is an initiation into the school of power. No one can actually graduate from the school of power. You will always need more power in your journey through life, and the more power you connect with, the greater your exploits.

For instance, the disciples were filled with the power

of the Holy Ghost on the day of Pentecost, but as their apostolic journey began and they were met with the demand of their ministry, they had to be refilled with greater power for effective ministry. The Bible says,

> *And with great power gave the apostles witness of the resurrection of the Lord Jesus: and great grace was upon them all.*
>
> *Acts 4:33*

The truth is: You can be filled and refilled with the power from on high. There is no end to being empowered and re-empowered. However, you must have a thirst, hunger, craving and longing for the power from on high. God is always willing and ready to fill you with His power, if only you are ready and willing to receive.

In 1976, I was baptised in the Holy Spirit, with the evidence of speaking in tongues. I am eternally grateful to God for granting me access to the power available in Holy Ghost baptism. Since then, I have asked God to refill me several times and I can tell you, it has been a wonderful experience!

The Resurrection Power

This is the Holy Ghost manifesting Himself in resurrection dimension. It is the demonstration of the mighty power of God. It brings to life everything dead in and around you and it is the ultimate power of God. The Bible says,

That I may know him, and the <u>power of his</u>
<u>resurrection</u>, and the fellowship of his sufferings,
being made conformable unto his death.

Philippians 3:10 (Emphasis mine)

The resurrection power is not just for selected individuals; rather, it is the will of God that all may experience this power. This is the same power that raised Jesus from the dead, and it supernaturally repositions believers into the realms of dominion and extraordinary works. The scripture says,

The eyes of your understanding being enlightened;
that ye may know what is the hope of his calling,
and what the riches of the glory of his inheritance
in the saints,

And what is the exceeding greatness of his power
to us-ward who believe, according to the working
of his mighty power,

Which he wrought in Christ, when he raised him
from the dead, and set him at his own right hand in
the heavenly places.

Ephesians 1:18-20

Clearly, the resurrection power is God's ultimate power on the earth. It performs the unimaginable and dominates death. It is the mighty power of God available for strange works on the earth. For instance, Jesus worked with mighty power in Ephesians 1:19 and He did mighty works. The Bible says,

And when he was come into his own country, he
taught them in their synagogue, insomuch that
they were astonished, and said, Whence hath this
man this wisdom, and these mighty works?

Matthew 13:54

The resurrection power is for the dominion and triumph of the saints and is called the quickening power of God. This is because it has the capacity to quicken your mortal body to become more like Christ, thereby making you live a divine life on the earth. It is written,

But if the Spirit of him that raised up Jesus from
the dead dwell in you, he that raised up Christ from
the dead shall also quicken your mortal bodies by
his Spirit that dwelleth in you.

Romans 8:11

Personally, my uttermost desire and longing is to begin to walk in this dimension of power now, more than ever. This is my prayer for you also.

The Power of the Tongue

Doubtless, there is power in your tongue! Your tongue has the power to create, as well as to destroy. The power of the tongue can also be referred to as the power of the spoken Word. Remember, at the beginning, God created everything in existence today by the power of the tongue. Everything that God commanded came to be (Genesis 1:1-26) and you were created in the same image and likeness of God. So, your tongue has also been empowered to bring to fulfilment what you desire. Scripture says,

> **Death and life are in the power of the tongue: and they that love it shall eat the fruit thereof.**
>
> *Proverbs 18:21*

The reason some people do not see results is because they are not saying anything. The power of the tongue comes to play only when you open your mouth to make declarations. It is written, **Thou shalt also decree a thing, and it shall be established unto thee...** (Job 22:28). You put the power of the tongue to work when you make biblical declarations, as God is always ready to confirm and perform every word backed up with power. The Bible says,

> **That confirmeth the word of his servant, and performeth the counsel of his messengers; that saith to Jerusalem, Thou shalt be inhabited; and to the cities of Judah, Ye shall be built, and I will raise up the decayed places thereof.**
>
> *Isaiah 44:26*

A story was once told of a mother who said to her child 'you are mad' and immediately, the child began to behave as a mad person. It is very important, therefore, to learn to use the power of the tongue cautiously, to <u>say</u> only what you want to <u>see</u>.

The Power in the Word

God's power is resident in His Word and God's Word is backed up by His power. Every word of scripture has power and capacity to produce results in the life of anyone who believes. Embedded in the Bible is the raw power of God which manifests in your life when you believe. It is written,

> *For the word of God is quick, and powerful, and sharper than any twoedged sword, piercing even to the dividing asunder of soul and spirit, and of the joints and marrow, and is a discerner of the thoughts and intents of the heart.*
>
> Hebrews 4:12

The Word of God is the carrier of God's power! It can overturn every situation and circumstance in a man's life. It has the capacity to bring the devil under your feet, sanctify you to live a holy life and enable you live a life of triumph. However, you can only gain access to the power in the Word through revelation, which comes from studying and meditating on the Word. The Bible says,

> *Let the word of Christ dwell in you richly in all wisdom; teaching and admonishing one another in psalms and hymns and spiritual songs, singing with grace in your hearts to the Lord.*
>
> Colossians 3:16

When you allow the Word of God to dwell in you, it will empower you with the wisdom to live holy, thereby granting you access to more power through deeper insight from the Word. It is written,

> *And the very God of peace sanctify you wholly; and I pray God your whole spirit and soul and body be preserved blameless unto the coming of our Lord Jesus Christ.*
>
> *1 Thessalonians 5:23*

God's Word is the fountain of God's power! His Word searches through your heart, breaks the barriers off your path and destroys every affliction of the devil. God's Word is a vital force of power for the triumph of every believer on the earth. Scripture says,

> *Is not my word like as a fire? saith the LORD; and like a hammer that breaketh the rock in pieces?*
>
> *Jeremiah 23:29*

However, you must understand that it is the same Holy Spirit that grants you access to the Word, revelation and power in the Word. Without the Holy Spirit, your access to the power in the Word will be futile.

Oh! How the body of Christ desperately needs greater access to the power in the Word today more than ever!

The Power in the Name of Jesus

This is another dimension of power. The name of Jesus is full of power. Everything in heaven and on earth is subject to the name of Jesus. It has the power to bring salvation and to deliver from every oppression of the devil. The name of Jesus is required for answers to prayers; every other name in heaven and on earth bows to that name. It is written,

> *That at the name of Jesus every knee should bow, of things in heaven, and things in earth, and things under the earth;*
>
> *And that every tongue should confess that Jesus Christ is Lord, to the glory of God the Father.*
>
> *Philippians 2:10-11*

The name of Jesus is your defence in the day of trouble. Every situation and circumstance bows to the name of Jesus. Some people are oppressed by the enemy and remain in struggles because they do not put to work the power in the name of Jesus. Difficult situations are dissolved, chains are broken and people are set free by the power in the name of Jesus.

A testimony was once shared of a man who was on the high sea when the boat capsized. He screamed, 'Jesus, I refuse to die'! Immediately, a supernatural hand held him until a rescue boat came.

It is written,

> *The name of the LORD is a strong tower: the righteous runneth into it, and is safe.*
>
> *Proverbs 18:10*

Also, it is written,

And these signs shall follow them that believe; In my name shall they cast out devils; they shall speak with new tongues;

Mark 16:17

In the name of Jesus, you have the authority to cast out devils and that name answers anywhere, in any situation and at any time. However, as with all other dimensions of power, you need the power at salvation before the power in the name of Jesus can work effectively for you. This is because the name of Jesus only answers to those who believe in it.

The Power to get Wealth

The power to get wealth is yet another dimension of power. You cannot encounter wealth in the Kingdom without power. It is this power from on high that multiplies the works of your hand, teaches you where to invest and what to engage in, in order to get wealth. Without the power to get wealth, people tend to work in futility. It is written,

But thou shalt remember the Lord thy God: for it is he that giveth thee power to get wealth, that he may establish his covenant which he sware unto thy fathers, as it is this day.

Deuteronomy 8:18

There are so many people who toil day and night, yet have next to nothing to show for their labour. This is because they have not encountered the power for wealth. When the power to get wealth comes upon a man, he produces maximum results with little effort because he is backed up by a divine power that cannot fail. The power to get wealth releases God's blessings on the works of one's hand, thereby resulting in supernatural increases.

The Power in the Sanctuary

There is power in the sanctuary, which is also the temple of God and the gathering together of spirits. Whenever believers gather together in one accord, power is present to break off every hold of the devil, as well as set free the captives. The Bible says that where two or three are gathered in God's name, He is in their midst (Matthew 18:20) and wherever God is, His power resides. The Psalmist said,

> *O God, thou art my God; early will I seek thee: my soul thirsteth for thee, my flesh longeth for thee in a dry and thirsty land, where no water is;*

> *To see thy power and thy glory, so as I have seen thee in the sanctuary.*

> *Psalm 63:1-2*

Whenever you appear in God's presence, don't just go casually. Attend church services, prayer meetings and every spiritual gathering with the aim of encountering the power from on high. It is this power that is responsible for supernatural manifestations in such places.

The disciples were gathered together praising, worshipping and praying when they encountered power from on high (Acts 2:1-4). That is why the Bible says we should not forsake the assembly of believers (Hebrews 10:25), because in that place of fellowship, there is power available to break every yoke, loose the band of wickedness and release to you your inheritance in Christ Jesus. The Bible says,

> *But upon mount Zion shall be deliverance, and there shall be holiness; and the house of Jacob shall possess their possessions.*
>
> *Obadiah 17*

Never allow anything discourage you from constantly attending church services, because it is a place of power.

The Power of the Gospel

Another dimension of power is the power of the gospel. The gospel of Christ is the power of God. The written gospel, when shared with others, has the power to bring salvation and restoration to the lives of those who believe and at the same time, empower the one witnessing to others. The Word of God says,

> *For I am not ashamed of the gospel of Christ: for it is the power of God unto salvation to every one that*

believeth; to the Jew first, and also to the Greek.

Romans 1:16

When Jesus sent out the 70 to witness, He gave them power to cast out every devil. On their return, they testified that even the devils were subject to them because of the power at work in them (Luke 10:17-19). The Bible says,

...he that winneth souls is wise.

Proverbs 11:30

Clearly, soul winning is a platform on which you can be empowered with the power from on high. When you win souls into the Kingdom, you please God well and He in turn empowers those who are faithful and diligent in His service, especially in soul winning. It is written,

... How beautiful are the feet of them that preach the gospel of peace, and bring glad tidings of good things!

Romans 10:15

Witnessing the gospel of Christ empowers. You are empowered with the Spirit of boldness to speak the Word of God to unsaved souls. The more you witness to others, the more empowered you become to dare and overcome every situation.

The Powers of the World to Come

This is another dimension of power that enables you to live the heavenly lifestyle here on earth. We are in the last days (Acts 2:17), and the church of God, which includes you and I, is ordained to take dominion over the world and the kingdom of darkness. However, the dominion of the church (believers) would be impossible without being empowered with the powers of the world to come. It is written,

> *And have tasted the good word of God, and the powers of the world to come,*
>
> Hebrews 6:5

When you are empowered with the powers of the world to come, you cannot be molested by the devil, because you have been empowered to torment devils. Everyone who gains access to the powers of the world to come lives the overcomer's lifestyle and the good news is that every believer can be empowered to this level. Even now, there is a yearning in my heart for a fresh baptism into this dimension of power. How about you?

As I conclude this chapter, it is worthy to note that all these dimensions of power have one source: The Holy Spirit. He is the custodian of the power from on high and He distributes it according to the demands of men. You can be empowered and re-empowered to whatever level you want, but you must crave it genuinely. Without your desperation for empowerment, it is impossible to be empowered and re-empowered by the Holy Spirit. The Bible says,

> *For by one Spirit are we all baptized into one body,*

> *whether we be Jews or Gentiles, whether we be*
> *bond or free; and have been all made to drink into*
> *one Spirit.*
>
> *1 Corinthians 12:13*

Also, it is written,

> *For through him we both have access by one Spirit*
> *unto the Father.*
>
> *Ephesians 2:18*

The power at salvation and that of the Holy Ghost must precede the receipt of the resurrection power. So, to enjoy the resurrection power, you must be born again and be baptised in the Holy Spirit with the evidence of speaking in tongues.

All these dimensions of power are available to you to enable you manifest your dominion in the journey of life. In subsequent chapters, we will discuss more on the Holy Ghost, who is the custodian of this power from on high.

3

Why We Need The Power Of The Holy Spirit

And we know that we are of God, and the whole world lieth in wickedness.

1 John 5:19

We live in an embattled world; a world full of wickedness. These wicked forces will neither bow to your religion, nor your daily church attendance; they will only bow to the power of God at work in your life. This is primarily why every believer needs to be empowered.

On your path to fulfilment of destiny, there are serpents and scorpions, but the good news is that God has made power available to overcome all the wickedness of the devil, and yet be unhurt! The following scripture is very revealing,

Behold, I give unto you power to tread on serpents and scorpions, and over all the power of the enemy: and nothing shall by any means hurt you.

Luke 10:19

Clearly, you must be empowered for conquest or destiny will remain at a risk.

There was a testimony of a cultist who came to our church sometime ago in Lagos, Nigeria. According to him, anyone he shook hands with would die. When he was sent to our church in 1993 to destroy, his powers were of no effect; rather, God tortured him from that time till 2013.

During one of our outreaches in 2013, he gave his life to Christ and got born again. In his testimony, he said:

I left my parent's house when I was in primary three. I have never been happy or happy with those who are rejoicing. I loved killing and shedding innocent blood.

Due to this nature, I joined a secret society called 'the blade', through a woman known as Mama Jane. We did many things which were not so clear to me. On my initiation day, I was given a blade to eat which I took and by midnight, I found myself in the meeting where an oath was taken after I was welcomed into the group.

From then, I became a destroyer of lives, until 1993, when I was given a mission to Living Faith Church a.k.a. Winners' Chapel, then in Iyana Ipaja, Lagos, Nigeria.

Naturally, when on a mission, we would appear to people outside in white, make it look like a white garment church, thereby dissuading them from coming into the church.

My duty was usually to command the blade in my hand to come out and cut people's lungs, intestines, etc. They won't die immediately, till they got home. When I got to Living Faith Church at Raji Oba Lagos, to do the same thing, I was caught up with fire which made me feel heat even when in an air-conditioned room.

Secondly, my mission was unaccomplished, and I could no longer see my gang members in the spirit. After many years, I met a sister on an evangelistic outreach on July 27, 2013, who preached Christ to me and invited me to church. She prayed with me and gave me a handbill. Throughout that night, I could not sleep.

That Sunday, I followed her to church and on Wednesday, I attended the service and partook of the Holy Communion. Immediately I took the Flesh and the Blood of Jesus Christ, the heat in me since 1993 ceased and I felt light and relieved. Those things I used to see at night stopped. I give glory to God for saving me! — **Mr. Dickson, O.**

Thank God for His power at work in His church that thwarted the plans of the enemy! The devil is called 'the wicked' (1 John 5:18). You do not have to do anything wrong to be his target. However, an encounter with the power from on high, which is a higher power, destroys every power or wicked forces against your life and destiny.

Please understand: Life is a personal race; no one has the capacity to run for another. You need a personal encounter with the power of the Holy Spirit for several reasons. These include, but not limited to the following:

To subdue your enemy: We are primarily in a power contest. Daily, the kingdom of darkness opposes the Kingdom of light. Thus, we need the power of the Holy Spirit to subdue these forces of darkness in order to possess our inheritances in Christ. The Bible reveals,

> *And from the days of John the Baptist until now the kingdom of heaven suffereth violence, and the violent take it by force.*
>
> Matthew 11:12

From the day a man is born till he breathes his last, there will always be battles to fight. For instance, there are people who do not like you for no justifiable reason and will therefore, want to bring you down at any cost. More so, we have our archenemy, the devil, who opposes us day and night; hence, the need for power.

However, these enemies are not just physical, they are primarily spiritual; but you must combat them spiritually in order to be victorious. From scriptures, it is clear that the spiritual controls the physical (John 3:31). So, until the war, which requires adequate empowerment is won spiritually, the battle against your enemies cannot be won in reality.

Truth is: As a believer, you are not of this world; hence, you will be opposed by the forces of this world. You definitely need a higher power to confront them and that power is released only through your desperation for it. The Holy Spirit is always available to release God's power in higher degrees to those who ask Him genuinely, in faith.

Think on this: When a child is confronted outside the home by a person who seems stronger or older, he or she rushes back home to seek refuge in an older sibling, parent or relation. This is because children are confident that the presence of a stronger person makes them untouchable.

Similarly, when a man is empowered from on high, he becomes untouchable, unmolestable and indestructible. His confidence is boosted and he can subdue every mountain. God speaking concerning David said,

I have found David my servant; with my holy oil have I anointed him:
With whom my hand shall be established: mine arm also shall strengthen him.
The enemy shall not exact upon him; nor the son of wickedness afflict him.
And I will beat down his foes before his face, and plague them that hate him.
But my faithfulness and my mercy shall be with him: and in my name shall his horn be exalted.
Psalm 89:20-24

From the above scripture, it is clear that when David was anointed, he became empowered. With this power, he was able to subdue his enemies and to beat down his foes before his face. It is written,

> *Out of the mouth of babes and sucklings hast thou ordained strength because of thine enemies, that thou mightest still the enemy and the avenger.*
>
> *Psalm 8:2*

Remember, the devil is our main enemy; he has always opposed the works of God in the life of man from the beginning. The Bible calls him our adversary, and he always goes around seeking whom he may devour (1 Peter 5:8). Thank God for the power of God that makes us triumphant in all things. Always remember,

> *And in nothing terrified by your adversaries...*
>
> *Philippians 1:28*

There was a time in my life when I was confronted with the spirit of fear. The Spirit of God quickened this scripture in my heart and by it, I was able to overcome.

It is impossible to live a triumphant life without power; but the good news is that God has not given us the spirit of fear, but of power, of love and of a sound mind. Therefore, that power from on high is available to every believer today, including you (2 Timothy 1:7).

Clearly, power is in degrees and no matter your level of empowerment presently, you need a greater level!

To fulfil your glorious destiny: By redemption, every believer has a glorious destiny in Christ. However, one of the reasons this has not become a reality in the lives of many is lack of adequate power from on high. It is written,

> *According as his divine power hath given unto us all things that pertain unto life and godliness, through the knowledge of him that hath called us to glory and virtue:*
>
> *2 Peter 1:3*

The truth is: All you require to fulfil your glorious destiny has been made available to you by God, but you cannot realise this without being endued with the power of the Holy Spirit. Think on this scripture,

> *For a great door and effectual is opened unto me, and there are many adversaries.*
>
> *1 Corinthians 16:9*

In the words of Dr. David O. Oyedepo, 'In everyman's promised land, there are giants'.

The fact that God has given you an inheritance does not mean that you have possessed it; there is usually a contest with unseen forces. Power is, therefore, required primarily to subdue these unseen forces. Read this scripture carefully,

> *Rise ye up, take your journey, and pass over the river Arnon: behold, I have given into thine hand*

> *Sihon the Amorite, king of Heshbon, and his land:*
> *begin to possess it, and contend with him in battle.*
> Deuteronomy 2:24

You cannot possess your possessions without contending in battle!

The full realisation of all the benefits of redemption calls for a fight and this can only be by divine strength, which is available only from God through enduement with power from on high. You shall not be robbed of that which rightfully belongs to you anymore!

To reign as kings on the earth: The success of any king is in the exercise of his power. Without power, a king would neither be recognised nor be functional. The Bible says,

> *And hast made us unto our God kings and priests:*
> *and we shall reign on the earth.*
> Revelation 5:10

David was anointed as king long before he began to reign on the throne. It was the power from on high, through the anointing on his life, that gave him his throne such that the people sang, 'Saul has slain a thousand and David ten thousand' (1 Samuel 18:7). He was able to subdue nations and kingdoms because of the power of God upon his life.

As a believer, you have been redeemed as a king unto God but you require power to reign victoriously.

Remember, Apostle Paul was so empowered that even demons attested to the fact that they knew him (Acts 19:15). Indeed, he reigned as a king on the earth! That is what God has ordained for you also. By the grace of God, you shall not miss it!

To take your redemptive blessing: It is written,

> *Saying with a loud voice, Worthy is the Lamb that was slain to receive power, and riches, and wisdom, and strength, and honour, and glory, and blessing.*
> *Revelation 5:12*

Here in the confirming verse, your redemptive blessings are clearly listed. It reveals that Christ died to receive for you power, riches, wisdom, strength, honour, glory and blessing. I strongly believe that it is not a coincidence that power is the first on the list. It is evident, therefore, that power is principal to your receiving all the other blessings of redemption listed above. So, without adequate power, you cannot take your redemptive blessings.

Power is in Degrees!

In subduing the enemy that is against your glorious destiny, the level of power you possess is crucial. It is not enough to be empowered, it is important to be adequately empowered. For instance, when the disciples could not cast out the demon from the possessed boy, Jesus attested to the fact that it was because they lacked enough power (Mathew 17:20-21). Jesus also affirmed that power is in degrees when He said,

> *When a strong man armed keepeth his palace, his goods are in peace:*
>
> *But when a stronger than he shall come upon him, and overcome him, he taketh from him all his armour wherein he trusted, and divideth his spoils.*
>
> *Luke 11:21-22*

In other words, contending for a strong man's possession will definitely be resisted, but when a stronger power comes, all opposition bows.

Some of the various degrees of power identified in scriptures include:

- **Power:** The moment a man receives Jesus as Lord and Saviour, power is released to enable such individual to genuinely acknowledge and repent of his/her sins and become a bonafide child of God. The Bible records,

> *But as many as received him, to them gave he power to become the sons of God, even to them that believe on his name.*
>
> *John 1:12*

However, beyond the power at salvation is the power that comes with the infilling of the Holy Spirit. It enables you to be an effective witness of Christ on earth. Without this power, you might still remain timid and unable to tell others about your salvation and the need for theirs. As it is written,

> *But ye shall receive <u>power</u>, after that the Holy Ghost is come upon you: and ye shall be witnesses unto me both in Jerusalem, and in all Judaea, and in Samaria, and unto the uttermost part of the earth.*
>
> Acts 1:8 (Emphasis mine)

However, you need to go beyond this to a deeper level of power. You need to get to a stage where you will confront oppositions with boldness and this advancement comes mainly through prayers. It is the intensity of your crave for empowerment that brings you to the next realm.

• **Great Power:** You need great power to be able to confront great oppositions. The battles of life are fierce, especially when you are out for Jesus, winning souls into the Kingdom. After the Apostles began witnessing the resurrection of Christ, they were threatened and persecuted. There was a need for re-empowerment, which they got on the altar of prayer. It is written,

> *And with <u>great power</u> gave the apostles witness of the resurrection of the Lord Jesus: and great grace was upon them all.*
>
> Acts 4:33 (Emphasis mine)

Life is in stages and the degrees of power you need to victoriously cross every stage differ. So, you need to upgrade your power level as you grow in your Christian life.

- **Exceeding Great Power:** This is yet another degree of power and you need it to command greater testimonies, signs and wonders. God's power is exceedingly great and unfathomable, and His exceeding great power is available to all who believe in the power of God to perform exceeding great works. It takes a higher degree of faith to manifest the exceeding greatness of God's power. The Bible says,

  And what is the <u>exceeding greatness of his power</u> to us-ward who believe, according to the working of his mighty power.
  Ephesians 1:19 (Emphasis mine)

  You gain access to this degree of power primarily through the revelation of the knowledge of the Word of God.

- **Mighty Power:** To walk in the realm of no limits, you need access to the mighty power of God. It was God's mighty power that brought Israel out of Egypt (Deuteronomy 9:29). Also, Jesus performed great miracles through the mighty power of God (Luke 9:43). God's mighty power is responsible for all the miraculous works on the earth, including raising of the dead. So, you need the mighty power of God to perform mighty works. It is written,

And what is the exceeding greatness of his power to us-ward who believe, according to the working of his <u>mighty power</u>.

Ephesians 1:19 (Emphasis mine)

The Kingdom of God is a Kingdom of show of power and the deeper your level of power, the greater your command over the affairs of life.

- **Glorious Power:** This degree of power strengthens you with might to live the heavenly lifestyle on the earth. You are endued to live above principalities, powers and rulers of darkness of this world, because God's glorious power surpasses all powers on the earth. I love this scripture,

Strengthened with all might, according to his <u>glorious power</u>, unto all patience and longsuffering with joyfulness.

Colossians 1:11 (Emphasis mine)

Oh, how I pray that God will keep advancing His church from one degree of power to another, more than ever. This is my heart cry!

Please understand that God's power is for your benefit. God does not need this power to manifest, because He is all-powerful. However, you need to grow in the power of God to triumph in life, above all oppositions against your destiny.

From the foregoing, it is clear that the need for power in a growing dimension in a believer's life cannot be overemphasised. May you encounter the power from on high, the power of the Holy Spirit afresh, even as you read this book!

4

The Holy Spirit: His Person

Howbeit when he, the Spirit of truth, is come, he will guide you into all truth: for he shall not speak of himself; but whatsoever he shall hear, that shall he speak: and he will shew you things to come.

John 16:13

A person is identified as a self-conscious being, who has the ability to think, reason, make and act on a choice, have desires, emotions and can express his or herself. The Holy Spirit possesses all these and more; this is why we can to a large extent define His personality.

The Holy Spirit, who is also referred to in scriptures as the Holy Ghost, is the most valuable asset to Christian living. He helps in all areas of our lives. No Christian can do without the Holy Spirit in the journey of life; that is why there is need for a personal relationship with Him.

Among other things, the Holy Spirit strengthens our spirit-man, keeps our souls alive and gives the energy required to our bodies. He is in charge of the affairs of the Kingdom of God on the earth. He is the central figure in any breakthrough in life.

Just as His name implies, He has a holy nature, void of sin and unrighteousness and He cannot be seen. He is not an emotional feeling; yet, He can be felt and He also speaks both to our spirit and sometimes audibly (Romans 8:16). Even though He is Spirit that cannot be seen, that does not make His presence and manifestations on the earth of less effect.

There are some vital characteristics of the Holy Spirit that will help you understand better who He is. Let us examine some of them here:

He is a Person

The Holy Spirit according to scriptures is a 'He'. This is a pronoun used to describe someone whose name has already been mentioned. He possesses some obvious characteristics of a person, such as the ability to hear, speak, answer questions and be grieved or vexed. He also teaches and searches even the deep things of God. The Bible says,

> *Howbeit when he, the Spirit of truth, is come, he will guide you into all truth: for he shall not speak of himself; but whatsoever he shall hear, that shall*

he speak: and he will shew you things to come.

John 16:13 (Emphasis mine)

The Bible also records that the Holy Spirit has a hand and He carries a fan and unquenchable fire, to purge our system from every chaff and planting of the enemy and to present us whole and blameless before God. Read these scriptures carefully,

> *...He shall baptize you with the Holy Ghost, and with fire:*
>
> *Whose fan is in his hand, and he will thoroughly purge his floor, and gather his wheat into the garner; but he will burn up the chaff with unquenchable fire.*
>
> Matthew 3:11-12

Please understand: The Holy Spirit has the ability to speak audibly to the heart of man because He is our eternal Guide; He also sees farther than you can ever see. He was there from the beginning and was part of creation, so He knows everything about life and knows what will happen every minute of the day. It is said of Him,

> *...God hath revealed them unto us by his Spirit: for the Spirit searcheth all things, yea, the deep things of God.*
>
> *For what man knoweth the things of a man, save the spirit of man which is in him? even so the things of God knoweth no man, but the Spirit of God.*
>
> 1 Corinthians 2:10-11

For instance, in the early church, the disciples were forbidden by the Holy Spirit to preach in some regions. It is written,

> **Now when they had gone throughout Phrygia and the region of Galatia, and were forbidden of the Holy Ghost to preach the word in Asia,**
>
> *Acts 16:6*

Really, when you have a personal relationship with the Holy Spirit, He can be closer to you than a physical friend, depending on how well you relate with Him. Just as communication builds relationship in the physical sense, constant communication with the Holy Spirit builds your relationship with Him. He is a person and you should endeavour to commune with Him regularly as you would to a friend.

Personally, I usually encourage believers to endeavour to pray in tongues for a minimum of 30 minutes daily. This, I have found to be very helpful in building a strong relationship with the Holy Spirit.

He is the Third Person in the Trinity

Scripturally, there is the Godhead, which is Trinity. There is God the Father, God the Son (Jesus) and God the Holy Spirit. The Holy Spirit is the third in the hierarchy, but that does not place Him as the least, because the Bible clearly states that these three are one. Scripture says,

For there are three that bear record in heaven, the
Father, the Word, and the Holy Ghost: and these
three are one.

1 John 5:7

Though these three are one, their functions differ.
The order in the Trinity is not necessarily an order of
importance, but an order of operations, manifestations
and revelations.

Clearly, each Person of the Godhead has individual
characteristics, responsibilities and operations, yet
none act independently or in opposition. For instance,
all plans or revelations come from the Father, through
the Son (Jesus), by the Holy Spirit. So, the Father (God)
initiates, the Son (Jesus) proclaims and the Holy Spirit
executes. It is so awesome that each member of the
Godhead has a distinct vital part; yet, they are closely
connected and therefore work together. It is written,

In the beginning God created the Heaven and the
earth.

And the earth was without form, and void; and
darkness was upon the face of the deep. And the
Spirit of God moved upon the face of the waters.
And God said ...

Genesis 1:1-3

It is so awesome that all through the account of
creation in Genesis, the Trinity was in operation
working together, but each performed their various

functions. God created everything by the Word (Jesus) while the Spirit of God moved to perform the action.

Jesus said,

> *Nevertheless I tell you the truth; It is expedient for you that I go away: for if I go not away, the Comforter will not come unto you; but if I depart, I will send him unto you.*
>
> *John 16:7*

Notably, the reign of the Holy Spirit began physically after Jesus departed from this world (Acts 1:8), although there were some manifestations of the Spirit before and during the time of Jesus on the earth (Psalm 51:11; Isaiah 63:10-11).

Like other members of the Trinity, the Holy Spirit is eternal, omnipotent, omniscient and sovereign. To understand His functions better, you need a revelation of the Word because the Holy Spirit cannot be understood just with the human mind. Therefore, as you study the Word of God, constantly seek for a greater revelation of the Holy Spirit and His operations to you.

He is the Spirit of Truth

The Holy Spirit is also the Spirit of truth. He is the revealer of the hidden secrets of God and discerner of the thoughts and intents of the heart. Jesus said,

> *Howbeit when he, the Spirit of truth, is come, he will guide you into all truth: for he shall not speak*

of himself; but whatsoever he shall hear, that shall he speak: and he will shew you things to come.

John 16:13

Since God the Father, the Son and the Holy Spirit are one, they have the same attributes. For instance, it is impossible for God to lie (Hebrews 6:18), so also it is impossible for the Holy Spirit to lie. Jesus said whatever He speaks is the truth, because He does not speak of His own accord or intuition, but as He hears from the Father, so He speaks. That means whatsoever He speaks is true because God cannot lie (Numbers 23:19). The Bible says,

...It was impossible for God to lie...

Hebrews 6:18

Also, it is written,

This is he that came by water and blood, even Jesus Christ; not by water only, but by water and blood. And it is the Spirit that beareth witness, because the Spirit is truth.

1 John 5:6

Take a closer look at these two scriptures,

...Thy word is truth.

John 17:17

...It is the Spirit that beareth witness, because the Spirit is truth.

1 John 5:6

Really, the Holy Spirit connects us to the right Word, thereby empowering us for triumphant living.

He is our Intercessor

'To intercede' according to the *Cambridge Advanced Learner Dictionary* means 'to use your influence to persuade someone in authority to save someone else from punishment or to obtain forgiveness for the person'.

This is true of the Holy Spirit, but He does more than obtain forgiveness for us; He also helps our weaknesses in prayer.

Sometimes, when we pray, we have difficulty with <u>what</u> to say or <u>how</u> to correctly present our requests to God. At other times, we might not pray according to the will of the Father, because there is always a right way to pray. That was why the disciples told Jesus to teach them to pray (Luke 11:1). However, when the Holy Spirit intercedes on our behalf, it is always the right way, with the right words and at the appropriate time. It is written,

> *Likewise the Spirit also helpeth our infirmities: for we know not what we should pray for as we ought: but the Spirit itself maketh intercession for us with groanings which cannot be uttered.*
>
> *And he that searcheth the hearts knoweth what is the mind of the Spirit, because he maketh*

intercession for the saints according to the will of God.

Romans 8:26-27

This explains why every prayer prompted by the Holy Spirit is usually an answered prayer, because He always knows the mind of God concerning us at every point in time. Also, the Holy Spirit searches the deep things of God, and brings answers to our requests. Indeed, a believer cannot intercede effectively without the help of the Holy Spirit.

Oswald Chambers said, 'If we rely on the Holy Spirit, we shall find that our prayers become more and more inarticulate; and when they are inarticulate, reverence grows deeper and deeper'. When your prayer becomes more *inarticulate* in this way, answers are more guaranteed.

He is the Believer's Seal

A seal is a mark of authority. It places a guarantee on a document or letter, indicating ownership and preventing it from being tampered with. In the same vein, the Holy Spirit is the believer's seal in all ramifications. Without the seal of the Holy Spirit, there is no evidence that you are born again. The Bible says the Spirit bears witness with our spirit that we are children of God (Romans 8:16).

When a person becomes born again, the Holy Spirit

becomes resident in him/her. Every believer is given the Holy Spirit, because He is the Spirit that confirms through an inner prompting or witness that you are a child of God (1 John 3:21).

Also, the seal of the Spirit is to protect you from all harms of the enemy and to give you your inheritance with other saints. The Bible says,

> *In whom ye also trusted, after that ye heard the word of truth, the gospel of your salvation: in whom also after that ye believed, ye were sealed with that holy Spirit of promise,*
>
> *Ephesians 1:13*

So, you are sealed with the Holy Spirit of promise! Henceforth, it is important that you become aware of this seal of the Holy Spirit upon you everywhere you go!

He is our Comforter

Before Jesus physically departed the earth, He saw that there was need for a helper; One who would stand as a guide, an advocate and majorly, a help for man. The inadequacies of man are limitless and the help of a higher power is required. It is written,

> *So I returned, and considered all the oppressions that are done under the sun: and behold the tears of such as were oppressed, and they had no comforter; and on the side of their oppressors there was power; but they had no comforter.*
>
> *Ecclesiastes 4:1*

When Jesus introduced the Holy Spirit, He called Him the Comforter. Among His mission on the earth is to help the believer through life, so we can live above the wickedness of the wicked. The Holy Spirit is to make our lives comfortable and 'to be comfortable' means to be restful; a state of 'sweatlessness'. As Dr. David Oyedepo puts it, 'The Comforter is the true name of the Holy Spirit and His ministry is to make living comfortable for us'. The Holy Spirit does this by removing stress from us. It is clearly stated,

> **And I will pray the Father, and he shall give you another Comforter, that he may abide with you for ever;**
>
> *John 14:16*

Notably, all that Jesus represented is what the Holy Spirit represents today. The good news is: You are neither redeemed to live a frustrated life, nor left to fate. The Holy Spirit is on the earth today to make living profitable for you by granting you directions and helps; but you have to ask Him! It is written,

> **But the Comforter, which is the Holy Ghost, whom the Father will send in my name, he shall teach you all things, and bring all things to your remembrance, whatsoever I have said unto you.**
>
> *John 14:26*

From now on, by the help of the Holy Spirit, and in

the name of Jesus, may all your sweat be turned to sweet, trials to triumphs, temptations to testimonies, labour to favour and depressions to great joy!

5

The Holy Spirit: His Manifestation And Evidence

But the manifestation of the Spirit is given to every man to profit withal.

1 Corinthians 12:7

Often times, many misunderstand this aspect of the Holy Spirit; they mistake the manifestation of the Holy Spirit for His person. These manifestations are the perceptible, outward, visible expressions to prove that the Holy Spirit is present; they are not who He is.

From scriptures, it is clear that the Holy Spirit manifests Himself through several mediums for the benefit of the body of Christ. Let us examine some of them briefly here:

The Holy Spirit as Water: One of the forms through which the Holy Spirit manifests Himself is water; and water is known for cleansing, refreshing and to quench thirst, among other things. It is written,

> And it shall come to pass afterward, that I will pour out my spirit upon all flesh; and your sons and your daughters shall prophesy, your old men shall dream dreams, your young men shall see visions:
>
> And also upon the servants and upon the handmaids in those days will I pour out my spirit.
>
> Joel 2:28-29 (Emphasis mine)

From the above scripture, you will agree with me that you can only pour something that is of a liquid substance. Jesus said,

> ...If any man thirst, let him come unto me, and drink.
>
> He that believeth on me, as the scripture hath said, out of his belly shall flow rivers of living water.
>
> (But this spake he of the Spirit, which they that believe on him should receive: for the Holy Ghost was not yet given; because that Jesus was not yet glorified).
>
> John 7:37-39 (Emphasis mine)

The Holy Spirit is likened to a river of flowing water, which among other things is supposed to quench the thirst of every soul that comes to Him. 'A thirst' connotes desperation. Therefore, the Spirit as water is an answer to a desperate cry to satisfy the longings of your soul and to fulfil God's plan for your life.

Also, the Holy Spirit manifesting in you as a river

of living water requires that others benefit from every gift He has deposited in you. The gifts of God are to be engaged to profit others. Remember, stagnant water stinks; so it is when the gifts of the Holy Spirit in an individual are not fully expressed.

The Holy Spirit as Fire: The Holy Spirit appeared like cloven tongues of fire in Acts 2:3,

> *And there appeared unto them cloven tongues like as of fire, and it sat upon each of them.*
> *(Emphasis mine)*

This fire is to purge us from every work of the devil and to present us pure and spotless before God. Jesus speaking concerning the Holy Spirit said He has a fan and a fire and will thoroughly purge his floor (Matthew 3:11-12).

Since we are the temple of the Holy Spirit and He cannot dwell in a defiled or polluted environment, He ensures that He cleans where He resides, and He does that by manifesting as fire. The Bible says,

> *But who may abide the day of his coming? and who shall stand when he appeareth? for he is like a refiner's fire, and like fullers' soap:*
>
> *And he shall sit as a refiner and purifier of silver: and he shall purify the sons of Levi, and purge them as gold and silver, that they may offer unto the LORD an offering in righteousness.*
> *Malachi 3:2-3*

However, this fire is not just to purify the believer, but also to burn the chaff from our lives. This chaff represents every planting of the devil meant to oppress and torment. It is written,

> *Whose fan is in his hand, and he will throughly purge his floor, and gather his wheat into the garner; but he will burn up the chaff with unquenchable fire.*
>
> *Matthew 3:12*

As the Holy Spirit begins to manifest in your life more than ever, expect every enemy tormenting your life and destiny to be burnt with His unquenchable fire!

The Holy Spirit as Oil: Another way through which the Holy Spirit manifests is the oil. The oil represents the anointing of the Holy Spirit and this anointing quickens His works and presence in a man's life. The effect of the oil of the Spirit is primarily to _empower_ and _enthrone_. In scriptures, before any king is enthroned, such person is usually anointed (1 Samuel 16:1, 13). This is to empower the person for the throne or office.

For instance, when King Saul was anointed with oil, the Spirit in the oil turned him into another man, such that he prophesied with the prophets. Read this scripture carefully,

> *Then Samuel took a vial of oil, and poured it upon his head, and kissed him, and said, Is it not because the LORD hath anointed thee to be captain over his inheritance?*
>
> *And the Spirit of the LORD will come upon thee,*

and thou shalt prophesy with them, and shalt be turned into another man.

And when they came thither to the hill, behold... the Spirit of God came upon him, and he prophesied among them.

...Then the people said one to another... Is Saul also among the prophets?

1 Samuel 10:1, 6, 10 – 11(b)

It was when he was anointed with oil that the Spirit came upon him. This proves that the Spirit can manifest Himself in the oil. It is written,

The Spirit of the Lord GOD is upon me; because the LORD hath <u>anointed</u> me to...

Isaiah 61:1 (Emphasis mine)

When a believer is anointed with oil, the Spirit of the Lord in the oil or the anointing comes upon such an individual for dominion over the adversary. Personally, I use the anointing oil regularly and can therefore testify that indeed, it works!

The Holy Spirit as Rain: Another manifestation of the Holy Spirit is as the rain of God upon the end-time Church. It is written,

Ask ye of the LORD rain in the time of the latter <u>rain</u>; so the Lord shall make bright clouds, and give them showers of <u>rain</u>, to every one grass in the field.

Zechariah 10:1 (Emphasis mine)

Among other things, this rain brings increase. In Acts 2:41, after the rain of the Holy Spirit came upon the believers in the early church, about 3,000 souls were added to them in one day. Also, as seen in Joel 2:28-32, with the rain of the Spirit comes restoration of glory and dignity of the church; it also brings deliverance.

The Holy Spirit as Dove: In Matthew 3:16, the Holy Spirit descended on Jesus like a dove. This, among other things, symbolises gentleness, stability, peace and progress; and that moved Jesus to His next phase in life and ministry. The Bible says,

> *And straightway coming up out of the water, he saw the heavens opened, and the Spirit like a dove descending upon him:*
>
> *And there came a voice from heaven, saying, Thou art my beloved Son, in whom I am well pleased.*
> *Mark 1:10-11 (Emphasis mine)*

Clearly, the Holy Spirit is a peaceful Spirit and as such, will not coerce you to do His will. Also, His presence in any man's life comes with peace because, as earlier stated, His presence is meant to make life comfortable for you.

In the words of Pastor Enoch A. Adeboye: 'It is hard to describe God and the Holy Spirit but He can be described as a mighty rushing wind, fire, oil or a mighty river'.

I want to state clearly at this point that, having listed some of the ways through which the Holy Spirit manifests Himself to you, it is important to note that He is neither any of these mediums, nor subjected to them. The Holy Spirit is a person.

Evidences Of The Holy Spirit In You

When the Holy Spirit is in you, what are the evidences, proofs or signs? Let us examine some of them briefly here:

Speaking in New Tongues: When God sent you to this world, you were born into a particular nation and an ethnic group with a distinct mother tongue. This serves as an identity to show where you are from. Likewise, the baptism of the Holy Spirit and speaking in new tongues are for born again believers.

It was revealed to Prophet Isaiah that God will speak to His people with another tongue different from the ones known. As it is written,

> *For with stammering lips and <u>another tongue</u> will he speak to this people.*
> *Isaiah 28:11 (Emphasis mine)*

Jesus confirmed this when He appeared to His disciples before His ascension. He said, *And these signs shall follow them that believe... they shall speak with <u>new tongues</u>* (Mark 16:17, Emphasis mine).

Notably, speaking in new tongues is a sign that you believe in the resurrection of Jesus and an evidence of your baptism in the Holy Spirit. Just as the intonation and language a person speaks can tell his or her biological origin; likewise, speaking in tongues confirms your Kingdom citizenship.

At Pentecost, when the disciples were baptised in the Holy Spirit, they spoke in new tongues such that everyone who heard them knew that there was something different about their language. It is written,

> *And they were all filled with the Holy Ghost, and began to speak with other tongues, as the Spirit gave them utterance.*
>
> *Acts 2:4*

Tongues is a heavenly language that is peculiar to only Spirit-filled believers, and no one knows what you are saying except by the interpretation of the Holy Spirit who is the distributor of this language (1 Corinthians 14:2). Moreover, all through the Acts of Apostles, speaking in new tongues was the evidence that a person was born again and filled with the Holy Spirit.

When Peter was sent by God in a vision to Cornelius and his household, it was recorded that while Peter spoke the Word, the Holy Spirit fell upon all that heard. The evidence of His arrival was the speaking of new tongues as recorded in Acts 10:44-46,

While Peter yet spake these words, the Holy Ghost fell on all them which heard the word.

And they of the circumcision which believed were astonished, as many as came with Peter, because that on the Gentiles also was poured out the gift of the Holy Ghost.

For they heard them speak with tongues, and magnify God...

However, just as every language requires constant practice for mastery, so it is with speaking in tongues. You should practice constantly by exercising yourself in the Holy Spirit. The Bible says,

But ye, beloved, building up yourselves on your most holy faith, praying in the Holy Ghost.

Jude 20

Improved Prayer Life: Another vital evidence of the indwelling of the Holy Spirit is an improved prayer life. The Bible records in Romans 8:26 that the Holy Spirit helps our infirmities on the altar of prayer. Another word for 'infirmities' is 'weaknesses'. Without the help of the Holy Spirit on the altar of prayer, man will be limited as to what to say, how to say it and the effect of such prayers.

I have discovered that some people can be very active when it comes to other spiritual activities but when it is time to pray, the spirit of slumber overtakes them and renders their prayer life ineffectual. At other times, some people tend to be more alert after the prayer sessions are over. But why?, you may ask. This is primarily because they lack power on the prayer altar and this power can only be received through the help of the Holy Spirit. It is written,

> **And I will pour upon the house of David, and upon the inhabitants of Jerusalem, the spirit of grace and of supplications...**
>
> *Zechariah 12:10(a)*

One key area in which the Holy Spirit helps in improving our prayer lives is in **removing vain repetitions**. Sometimes, either for lack of words or what to pray about, it is possible to repeat words unnecessarily in prayers. Jesus teaching said,

> **But when ye pray, use not vain repetitions, as the heathen do: for they think that they shall be heard for their much speaking.**
>
> **Be not ye therefore like unto them: for your Father knoweth what things ye have need of, before ye ask him.**
>
> *Matthew 6:7-8*

The Father knows what we need even before we ask and the Holy Spirit searches the deep things of God to know His mind concerning us. This means there is no better person to help us in removing vain repetitions in prayers than the Holy Spirit.

The Holy Spirit also **strengthens us in prayer** by enabling us to pray for a longer period of time and with greater effect. It was the power of the Spirit at work in Jesus that enabled Him to pray the way He did. The Bible records that Jesus went in the power of the Holy Ghost and in one of His prayer sessions, He prayed till sweat dropped from Him like blood (Luke 22:44). Jesus was seen praying regularly during the night seasons, which can only be by supernatural strength. The Bible records,

> *And it came to pass in those days, that he went out into a mountain to pray, and continued all night in prayer to God.*
>
> *Luke 6:12*

Definitely, to pray effectively and keep the fire on the prayer altar burning, you need the Holy Spirit so He can supply you with needed strength in prayer.

Boldness in the Things of God: This is another evidence that the Holy Spirit dwells in you. The Spirit of God is the Spirit of boldness and this entails approaching every area of life with the understanding that the power of God is strongly behind you. As it is written,

> *For God hath not given us the spirit of fear; but of power, and of love, and of a sound mind.*
>
> *2 Timothy 1:7*

Also, it is written,

In whom we have boldness and access with confidence by the faith of him.

Ephesians 3:12

To be bold means to be brave, fearless and filled with an unusual confidence. For you to effectively fulfil God's plan for your life, you must be bold. This boldness does not mean just having a bold face; rather, it is the boldness of your spirit-man that keeps you active and fearless even when confronted with challenges.

When the disciples were filled with the Holy Spirit in the upper room, their boldness came alive. Peter who could not face a little girl when confronted the night Jesus was crucified (Matthew 26:71-72), spoke with boldness by the help of the Holy Spirit, such that 3,000 people became born again (Acts 2:14-41). At another instance, people noticed that Peter had been with Jesus because of the boldness he exhibited. It is written,

Now when they saw the boldness of Peter and John, and perceived that they were unlearned and ignorant men, they marvelled; and they took knowledge of them, that they had been with Jesus.

Acts 4:13

When you get filled with the Holy Spirit, He empowers your utterances. That is, He puts words in your mouth that you ordinarily would not think of; He enables you to speak those words as inspired by Him. For example, in the area of evangelism, when you are filled with the

Holy Spirit, He empowers you to witness for Jesus, enabling you to do or say what you ordinarily would not do or say. Scripture says,

> *For it is not ye that speak, but the Spirit of your Father which speaketh in you.*
>
> Matthew 10:20

To ascend the throne of grace also requires boldness. The Bible says, *Let us therefore come boldly unto the throne of grace, that we may obtain mercy, and find grace to help in time of need* (Hebrews 4:16).

Sometimes, the devil might want to weaken your confidence in God, by reminding you of things you have repented of and God has forgiven. But, with the empowerment of the Holy Spirit through the Word of God, you can boldly silence him of every accusation against you.

Increased Revelation: Revelation has to do with insight and this is an in-depth understanding of the mysteries in the Word of God. This is one other evidence of the Holy Spirit in you. The Bible is full of mysteries (Matthew 13:11; Luke 8:10), which contain treasures for profitable living. The Holy Spirit is our best guide in understanding the things of God, because He is the Revealer of the hidden secrets of God (John 16:13).

As recorded in Acts 8:30-31, the Ethiopian Eunuch read the book of Isaiah, but was unable to understand

it, because he had no access to the Spirit of revelation.
It is written,

> *Howbeit when he, the Spirit of truth, is come, he*
> *will guide you into all truth: for he shall not speak*
> *of himself; but whatsoever he shall hear, that shall*
> *he speak: and he will shew you things to come.*
>
> John 16:13

The Holy Spirit gives us understanding of the Word
of God which is called revelation or rhema. It is this
revelation that gives us authority over the powers of
the devil, because a man is as strong as the level of
revelation at work in him. The devil will only bow
to the revelation of the Word you put to work; this is
very critical! In the words of Dr. David O. Oyedepo,
'Revelation is the bedrock of every revolution; it is the
greatest asset to a life of exploits'.

It is very important to understand that it is not
enough to have a onetime revelation; you need an ever-
increasing dimension of revelation. That is why you
need to be in constant fellowship with the Holy Spirit.
Smith Wigglesworth once said: 'I never get out of bed in
the morning without having communion with God in
the Spirit'. Isn't that revealing?

A constant communion with God in the Spirit entitles
you to divine secrets, because it brings closeness and in
human sense, you can only reveal secrets to those you
have a close relationship with. The closer you are to the

Holy Spirit, the deeper He reveals to you the treasures in scriptures. As John MacArthur said: 'Apart from the Holy Spirit, the Bible will utterly fail to penetrate and transform the human heart. With the Spirit of God comes illumination – true understanding of what has been written'.

The Holy Spirit grants us in-depth revelation of the Word through desperation of the heart and accurate sensitivity to His voice when studying the Word. Don't just read the Bible like a story book, journal or history book; those who do, never get much out of it. To gain revelation and increase in it, you must engage in a spirited search so as to find something. However, for your search to be productive, you need the help of the Holy Spirit.

As I conclude this chapter, I pray that the manifestation and evidence of the Holy Spirit in your life shall become stronger from now, more than ever!

The Holy Spirit:
His Mission

But the Comforter, which is the Holy Ghost,
whom the Father will send in my name, he shall
teach you all things, and bring all things to your
remembrance, whatsoever I have said unto you.

John 14:26

The Holy Ghost is the facilitator of every great plan of
God on the earth. He is the One behind the manifestation
of God's plan for the believer, which among others is to
terminate shame.

Really, the Holy Ghost is your senior partner in
the journey of life; without Him, Christianity will be
mere religious frustration. He is your God-ordained
Helper in the adventure of life. He is the most reliable,
dependable and indispensable. He gives real value to
redemption and makes living profitable. It is written,

But the manifestation of the Spirit is given to every

man to profit withal.

1 Corinthians 12:7

The mission of the Holy Spirit includes, but is not limited to the following:

Grants Believers Access To Divine Power

Power is the only language that the devil understands and it is what distinguishes one believer from another. 1 Corinthians 4:20 states, 'The Kingdom of God is not in words, but in power'. In this Kingdom, it is your level of power that determines your dominion on the earth, and the Holy Spirit is your access to this power.

Before Jesus' ascension, He told the disciples to wait for an infilling with the Holy Spirit, which guarantees their access to power on the earth. The Bible records, **And, behold, I send the promise of my Father upon you: but tarry ye in the city of Jerusalem, until ye be endued with power from on high** (Luke 24:49).

The Holy Spirit is the custodian of God's power and as such, it is through Him we gain access to divine power. The Bible states,

> **But ye shall receive power, after that the Holy Ghost is come upon you...**

Acts 1:8

Also, it is written,

> **It is the spirit that quickeneth; the flesh**

profiteth nothing...

John 6:63

To 'quicken' means to 'empower' and from the above, it is clear that empowerment does not come from the flesh, but the Spirit. Even Jesus needed to be empowered by the Spirit for effective ministry on the earth. It was written concerning Him,

> **How God anointed Jesus of Nazareth with the Holy Ghost and with power: who went about doing good, and healing all that were oppressed of the devil; for God was with him.**

Acts 10:38

With the anointing of the Holy Spirit comes power, which is our access to mighty works and fulfilment of our mission on the earth. Without the power of the Holy Spirit at work in you, life will be difficult and destiny, insecure. You cannot afford to live your life without power, because in your personal encounter with the power of God lies the fulfilment of your destiny and also the liberation of many lives connected to you. Remember: You are not only saved for your benefit, but also to be used of God to liberate others from the works of darkness. It is written,

> **Then he answered and spake unto me, saying, This is the word of the Lord unto Zerubbabel, saying, Not by might, nor by power, but by my spirit, saith the Lord of hosts.**

Zechariah 4:6

True power cannot be gotten by might or connections with human sources, but by the Spirit of God. Anything that the devil or man gives is temporal and inferior to what the Holy Spirit gives. Therefore, beware! Do not seek earthly or demonic powers; crave the power that comes from above, because it is the only way to dominate principalities and the rulers of dark places of this world.

Convicts The World of Sin

From the beginning, man was born in sin. According to 1 Corinthians 15:22, every man born of a woman inherited the sins of Adam; but the good news is that Jesus our Messiah died to cleanse the world from sin. From scriptures, we understand that the god of this world, who is the devil, has blinded the eyes of many that they might not realise or come to terms with their need for repentance (2 Corinthians 4:4).

The Holy Spirit, through His convicting ability, pricks our conscience to help us see the need for salvation. No one can save any man except through the help of the Holy Spirit. It is the Spirit that purges our conscience of every dead work (Hebrews 9:14).

How do you explain a hardened criminal or herbalist waking up one morning and in his sinful and wicked state, realises that there is something missing in his life and therefore, decides to run to the saving power of the cross? Yes, it might be that he must have been preached to by someone years, months or days back, but those words alone have no power to save, without the Holy Spirit at work. It is written,

> **And when he is come, he will reprove the world of sin, and of righteousness, and of judgment:**
>
> *John 16:8*

The 3,000 people who got saved on the day of Pentecost did not receive salvation just because of the wonderful message Peter preached or his eloquence. Those might be important, but not as significant as the prompting of the Holy Spirit. It was recorded that they were 'pricked in their heart'. This pricking in their hearts is the convicting power of the Holy Spirit. Read this,

> **Now when they heard this, they were pricked in their heart, and said unto Peter and to the rest of the apostles, Men and brethren, what shall we do?**
>
> *Acts 2:37*

There is this fascinating testimony of a notorious herbalist, who had tormented the city for years and even the government was unable to arrest him. However, what no man could do, the Holy Spirit did sweatlessly. He testified:

I lived as an herbalist for 40 years. I was the second-in-command in the whole world. I had a flying carpet and a moving chair to travel anywhere in the world.

I was popularly known as 'Baba Onigba', by the media. Even government officials feared me. I was rich, married to nine wives and lived in a four-storey building with a bunker at Meiran, Lagos, Nigeria. In fact, I had everything I needed.

During the time of Governor Marwa's Operation Sweep, the security officers opened fire (gunshots) for five days on my house to arrest me, but they were unsuccessful. Whenever they tried to arrest me, the officials never returned. It was only the God of Bishop David Oyedepo that arrested me.

I lost seven of my wives and 13 children and I became crippled. For 23 days, I crawled like Nebuchadnezzar. While I was in Ota General Hospital, the Winners' pastor in my neighbourhood visited me and told me once again to give my life to Jesus Christ. On July 26, 2013, the pastor came with anointing oil and anointed me.

Thereafter, he asked me for the tools in my possession; I told him I had a marine wife – she was the queen of the river. The pastor took her pictures, all my charms and the mortar I had and burnt them.

Today I am saved; I can walk and I have surrendered everything to God. I thank God for what He has done for me! — **Taiwo, A.**

Clearly, this testifier was arrested by the power of

God and he surrendered his life to Christ. So, the Holy Spirit specialises in convicting men of sin and bringing them to repentance. Therefore, next time you embark on evangelism for Jesus Christ, be conscious of the fact that the Holy Spirit is the Lord of the harvest and He is in charge of convicting souls. With this understanding, you can employ His help by completely handing over to Him the souls you preached to and watch Him bring a bountiful harvest.

Reconciles Men Back To God

The word 'reconcile' means to find a way through which two situations or beliefs that are opposite to each other can agree and exist together. God is ever holy, while man's sinful nature makes both God and man opposite of each other. Hence, the need for reconciliation of man with God. The sacrifice of Jesus on the cross bridged that gap between God and man, thereby creating opportunity for holiness – spirit, soul and body (Galatians 5:17).

However, the union between God and man on the earth would be impossible without the help of the Holy Spirit. One of the core missions of the Holy Spirit, therefore, is to reconcile men back to God through the preaching of Jesus Christ and God's love for humanity. It is written,

> **And all things are of God, who hath reconciled us to himself by Jesus Christ, and hath given to us the**

> *ministry of reconciliation;*
>
> *To wit, that God was in Christ, reconciling the world unto himself, not imputing their trespasses unto them; and hath committed unto us the word of reconciliation.*
>
> 2 Corinthians 5:18-19

God reconciled the world to Himself by sacrificing Jesus Christ on the cross and He has commissioned believers to reconcile others outside of the fold, through the power in the message of Christ (Mathew 28:19-20). The boldness to begin and continue this mission of reconciliation is gotten through the empowerment of the Holy Spirit.

You will recall that in Acts 2, the emphasis was on evangelism after the disciples were empowered. The power from on high is not to be left dormant, but it is for the purpose of becoming an effective witness of Jesus, His resurrection power and God's love for humanity.

Also, it was after that empowerment that Peter could preach a historic message, leading to the salvation of 3,000 souls. Before then, he was a timid disciple, who denied Jesus at the mere instance of opposition. After he was empowered, he spoke the Word with boldness and authority. The Bible says,

> *And with great power gave the apostles witness of the resurrection of the Lord Jesus: and great grace was upon them all.*
>
> Acts 4:33

It is the Holy Spirit who gives utterance, by giving the right word for every circumstance of life (Psalm 81:10; Luke 21:15). T.L Osborn said: 'There is only one purpose of Pentecost; that is, to effectively evangelise lost souls'. Without the power of the Holy Spirit, reconciliation of men would be impossible. This is because the devil does not want anyone to be saved, but with the power of God, unbelievers are rescued from the clutches of the devil. It is written,

> **The Lord is not slack concerning his promise, as some men count slackness; but is longsuffering to us-ward, not willing that any should perish, but that all should come to repentance.**
>
> *2 Peter 3:9*

The truth is: God will use human instruments to preach salvation to men. Therefore, you must be willing and obedient to the will of God, by committing yourself and your best to the reconciliation of men. As it is written,

> **Let us go forth therefore unto him without the camp, bearing his reproach.**
>
> *Hebrews 13:13*

Understand that: To be a successful Christian, who is obedient to God, you must do the will of God, which is soul winning (John 15:5). Your fruitfulness in your walk with God can only be guaranteed when you reconcile men to God.

Grants Access To Divine Guidance

My husband, Dr. David Oyedepo has always said: 'One wrong step can wreck a whole destiny'. With this in mind, the need to be guided by the Holy Spirit cannot be overemphasised. Divine guidance is your guarantee to endless triumphs and sweatless victories. To be guided by God means to be led and directed aright. This is evident in the lives of our covenant fathers – Abraham, Isaac, Jacob and others.

In Deuteronomy 32:12-14, there is a graphic picture of the benefits of divine guidance,

> *So the Lord alone did lead him, and there was no strange god with him.*
>
> *He made him ride on the high places of the earth, that he might eat the increase of the fields; and he made him to suck honey out of the rock, and oil out of the flinty rock;*
>
> *Butter of kine, and milk of sheep, with fat of lambs, and rams of the breed of Bashan, and goats, with the fat of kidneys of wheat; and thou didst drink the pure blood of the grape.*

The truth is: Without divine guidance, the journey of life can be most frustrating. For instance, when you travel to a new city, you might have difficulty moving around without a tour guide or a road map. But, with the aid of technology today, there are softwares such as GPRS, Infrared and even Google maps, which make locating a place easier. So it is with the Holy Spirit. Any attempt to go through life without Him will lead to frustration. It is written,

> *Howbeit when he, the Spirit of truth, is come, he will guide you into all truth...*
>
> *John 16:13*

The Holy Spirit is our guide to every truth we need to be successful in life. There are several ways through which the Holy Spirit guides; they include but are not limited to the following:

Through the Word: The Holy Spirit is the inspiration behind the written Word – the Bible. Thus, He can always speak to us through the Word and more often than not, that is the medium through which He speaks. Scripture says,

> *Thy word is a lamp unto my feet, and a light unto my path.*
>
> *Psalm 119:105*

Many years ago, my husband and I were praying on the next location to serve in the work of the ministry. We wanted to know if we were to move to Kaduna (Northern Nigeria) or stay where we were. In the course of the prayer session, God through the Holy Spirit flipped the pages of scriptures in my husband's Bible, and then the answer came, *...And the Lord said unto* *me, Arise, and go into Damascus; and there it shall be told thee of all things which are appointed for thee to do* (Acts 22:10). Kaduna, a type of Damascus, a place of persecution! That was how the mission in Kaduna started, which today is a force to reckoned with.

The Word of God is a vital tool in receiving directions from God and His Word is always true. There is nothing God tells you from scriptures that will not be fulfilled and with the Word, you cannot be confused. Also, several people have shared testimonies of how major incidents that would have been disasters were averted by following the guidance of the Holy Spirit through the Word.

However, to be guided by the Word, you must be sensitive and studious, because it is through Word study that you will discover what God is saying to you (Proverbs 4:20-22).

Through an Inner Witness: An inner witness means a prompting in your spirit-man, probably on a direction to take, what to say or do. The Spirit of God directs our spirit to do the will of God. The Bible says,

> *For what man knoweth the things of a man, save the spirit of man which is in him? even so the things of God knoweth no man, but the Spirit of God.*
>
> *Now we have received, not the spirit of the world, but the spirit which is of God; that we might know the things that are freely given to us of God.*
>
> *1 Corinthians 2:11-12*

Personally, I often receive and enjoy divine guidance on various issues of life through an inner witness.

An Audible Voice: The Holy Spirit has a voice and He speaks. The voice of the Spirit is the voice of guidance. He guides us by speaking the mind of God to us. The Holy Spirit speaks and shows us God's plan for our lives. It is written,

> *I was in the Spirit on the Lord's day, and heard behind me a great voice, as of a trumpet.*
>
> *Revelation 1:10*

Notably, the Holy Spirit is a speaking Spirit; unfortunately, many people are taking dangerous and risky steps in life because they cannot hear His voice. I pray that you will be able to hear His voice from now, more than before!

Through a Prophet or Priest: Prophets and priests are God's mouthpiece on the earth. He said, *I have also spoken by the prophets, and I have multiplied visions, and used similitudes, by the ministry of the prophets* (Hosea 12:10).

At this point, it is important for me to mention that you must beware of false and professional prophets, who always make a prey of believers. You shall not fall a victim to such!

At a point in Apostle Paul's ministry, he was told by the Holy Spirit through a prophet named Agabus not to go to Jerusalem because he would be ill-treated there (Acts 21:10-11).

However, for the Holy Spirit to direct you, there is need for spiritual sensitivity. If you are not alert in the spirit, you might not hear Him when He speaks (Revelation 1:10). Remember, He has a still small voice (1 Kings 19:12); so, to pick that voice, your spirit-man must be at alert. You will no longer miss His leading, in the name of Jesus!

In all these, you might be wondering how to differentiate the voice of the Holy Spirit from other voices or your intuition. This is very important because the fact that you had a prompting does not mean it is the Holy Spirit directing you towards a particular thing; it might be drawn from your own desire or passion.

There was a time in the early days of our ministry when my husband felt that God was leading him to establish the base of the ministry in Jos, Nigeria. After the send-forth service and impartations, he decided to seek a quiet place to worship God for the events of that day, when He heard God say, 'I was not the One you heard'.

According to my husband, it was a surprise to him because he felt God was the One leading him there; but God reminded him of how he had always wanted to live in Jos if opportune; He made clear to him that it was his desire he had heard. Thank God for spiritual sensitivity; he was able to realise that it was not God's will for him at that time to move the ministry to Jos.

How do you know when the Holy Spirit is leading you?

Consider the following:

His guidance brings peace: Peace is one of the attributes of the Holy Spirit (Galatians 5:22). Jesus also said, '... **My peace I give to you...**' (John 14:27). Whenever the Holy Spirit leads, there is always peace. Remember, God is not the author of confusion (1 Corinthians 14:33).

In fact, when you are about taking a step and you are not peaceful about it, that is a major indication that you need to exercise caution. This is because every of the Spirit's direction brings peace. It is written,

> *To give light to them that sit in darkness and in the shadow of death, to guide our feet into the way of peace.*
>
> *Luke 1:79*

Supernatural supplies: The Holy Spirit will not lead you to where He has not made provisions for you. No earthly father ever sends a child and leaves him to provide for himself. So, wherever the Holy Spirit leads, He makes supplies available. Read this scripture carefully,

> *The Lord is my shepherd; I shall not want.*
>
> *He maketh me to lie down in green pastures: he leadeth me beside the still waters.*
>
> *He restoreth my soul: he leadeth me in the paths of righteousness for his name's sake.*
>
> *Psalm 23:1-3*

He goes before, with and after the led: The Holy Spirit is omnipresent; He can be everywhere at the same time. Therefore, when He leads you, you can be sure that He is with you, ahead of you and even behind you. He is with you to keep company with you and give you prompt instructions, He is ahead of you to make every crooked way straight and to clear every evil off your path. He then goes after you to keep watch against enemies that might want to hurt you from behind. Isn't that wonderful? It is written,

> *Yea, though I walk through the valley of the shadow of death, I will fear no evil: for thou art with me; thy rod and thy staff they comfort me.*
>
> *Thou preparest a table before me in the presence of mine enemies: thou anointest my head with oil; my cup runneth over.*
>
> *Surely goodness and mercy shall follow me all the days of my life: and I will dwell in the house of the Lord for ever.*
>
> Psalm 23:4-6

Supernatural joy: The Holy Spirit is the Spirit of joy. There is no leading of the Spirit that is not accompanied with joy. Concerning Jesus, the Bible records that '**... Who for the joy that was set before Him...**' (Hebrews 12:2). Therefore, wherever He leads guarantees a joyful end. The Bible says,

> *Thou wilt shew me the path of life: in thy presence is*

fulness of joy; at thy right hand there are pleasures for evermore.

Psalm 16:11

Divine accomplishment: God does not have abandoned or unfinished projects; His missions are always accomplished. Apostle Paul, who enjoyed the leading ministry of the Holy Spirit in abundance in his ministry, said, **'...I have finished the race...'** (2 Timothy 4:7).

Jesus promised that **the comforter, will abide with you till the end** (John 14:16). So, the Holy Spirit helps you accomplish your mission in life. This is very exciting and fulfilling.

He Quickens Our Mortal Bodies

To 'quicken' means to 'strengthen' or 'make more active'. Our body without the revitalising help of the Spirit is subject to weakness. The Holy Spirit is our help and one of the ways He does that is by infusing our bodies with His own strength. The Holy Spirit is a life giver; He is divine and the strength of divinity surpasses that of humanity. Therefore, being engrafted in Him means you taking up His strength, in exchange for your weakness. Isn't that wonderful? The Bible says,

But if the Spirit of him that raised up Jesus from the dead dwell in you, he that raised up Christ from the dead shall also quicken your mortal bodies by his Spirit that dwelleth in you.

Romans 8:11

This scripture is one of my favourite passages in the Bible. Please beware: Your body is the temple of the Holy Spirit; therefore, sickness, disease, affliction and weakness are illegal there (1 Corinthians 6:16-20). The Bible records that light and darkness have nothing in common, and at the root of every affliction is the devil (John 1:5). Therefore, when the Holy Spirit dwells in you, He sweeps out every work of darkness from your body and makes it fit for Him to dwell because you are His temple. It is written,

> *I indeed baptize you with water unto repentance: but he that cometh after me is mightier than I, whose shoes I am not worthy to bear: he shall baptize you with the Holy Ghost, and with fire:*
>
> *Whose fan is in his hand, and he will throughly purge his floor, and gather his wheat into the garner; but he will burn up the chaff with unquenchable fire.*
>
> *Mathew 3:11-12*

The Holy Spirit has a mission of preserving your body, thereby rescuing you from the cause of sickness and disease, which is sin. Sin cannot inhabit wherever the Holy Spirit dwells. Therefore, sickness and disease have no legal right in your body when He is present. By Him dwelling in you, I decree your freedom now from every sickness, disease or discomfort that may want to ravage your body, in the name of Jesus! Right now, as you read this, the healing river is flowing and you can tap into it.

He Helps Us To Pray Aright

Without the help of the Holy Spirit, prayer can become mere religion. There is always a right way to everything and that includes prayer. At times, people complain of their prayers not being answered or that they experience dryness on the prayer altar. This may be because they have not employed the help of the Holy Spirit. As our God-ordained Helper, the Holy Spirit helps in all things including prayer. The Bible says,

> *Likewise the Spirit also helpeth our infirmities: for we know not what we should pray for as we ought: but the Spirit itself maketh intercession for us with groanings which cannot be uttered.*
>
> *And he that searcheth the hearts knoweth what is the mind of the Spirit, because he maketh intercession for the saints according to the will of God.*
>
> Romans 8:26-27

There is a difference between knowing what to say and saying it right. Examining your daily conversations, you may have valid points, but the presentation also matters. Just as packaging makes a whole lot of difference to the success of every product, the end result of every well-packaged prayer is an answer from heaven. This is why you need the help of the Holy Spirit.

He helps to package our prayer correctly for answers. Just like a good lawyer is known by his presentation, the Holy Spirit presents our case accurately to God, thereby ensuring answers.

Henceforth, as you engage the ministry of the Holy Spirit in your prayer life more than before, may your prayer life be reenergised and undergo right transformation, in Jesus name!

'The Holy Spirit illuminates the minds of people, makes us yearn for God, and takes spiritual truth and makes it understandable to us'

– Billy Graham

7

The Holy Spirit: His Mission II

But the Comforter, which is the Holy Ghost, whom the Father will send in my name, he shall teach you all things, and bring all things to your remembrance, whatsoever I have said unto you.

John 14:26

The primary mission of the Holy Ghost is to help the believer through the journey of life. In fact, His mission is to make our lives meaningful, impactful and profitable. No one can attain true success without His help, as there are always oppositions on every side.

To be guided by the Holy Spirit brings life, peace, joy and fulfilment. He gives you a strong assurance, even when it seems like the world is falling apart. Personally, I would not be anywhere today if I did not have Him as my Help, Guide, Counsellor and Friend. He teaches what you need to know so as to stay on top in this world, and also live in eternal glory.

In this chapter, I shall discuss some of His other missions.

He Makes Our Lives Comfortable

Life is full of challenges, but Jesus said, *...But be of good cheer; I have overcome the world* (John 16:33). One of the ways He overcame the world for you is by sending the Comforter (Holy Spirit) to make life on earth comfortable until He returns.

As the redeemed of the Lord, you are to be envied, not pitied. When the Holy Spirit dwells in you, He makes your life attractive. Everything about the Holy Spirit is unique; people may begin to ask you what it is that makes you glow; it is the presence of the Holy Spirit! It is written,

> *Even the Spirit of truth; whom the world cannot receive, because it seeth him not, neither knoweth him: but ye know him; for he dwelleth with you, and shall be in you.*
>
> *I will not leave you comfortless: I will come to you.*
> *John 14:17-18*

In one of the books on the Holy Spirit authored by Kenneth E. Hagin, he explained how his preaching became different after he received the infilling of the Holy Spirit. According to him, at that time, he was a young preacher in one of the early days of the

Baptist denomination. That was at the time when the understanding of the mission of the Holy Spirit was not really clear to many believers.

He knew that he needed a deeper understanding of the Word, but he did not know how, until he had an encounter with the Holy Spirit. It was such that whenever he ministered every Sunday, there was always something unique. This became clearer when someone who mocked the move of the Spirit in the Pentecostal Church confronted him and said, 'There is something different about your preaching these days'. Kenneth E. Hagin asked, 'Is it good or bad?' When he said 'good', he said he knew it was the Holy Spirit.

So, the Holy Spirit brings ease to life, family, ministry, career, and indeed every area of life. This, He does by making living comfortable for us (John 16:7).

He Helps Us Walk In Love

The truth is: It is impossible to truly walk in love without the help of the Holy Spirit. The world gives so many reasons you should not and indeed, cannot love. Moreover, with the trend of evil occurrences, you might begin to question if it is really necessary to love. Remember, however, that God is love and if you are His child, then, you must walk in His steps. One of the ways to walk in His steps is to learn to love (1 John 4:8, 16).

One primary area where the Holy Spirit helps to love is in our love for God, because that is the foundation of all other areas of love. If you love God, you will seek to please Him, love His Kingdom and love others.

Jesus said, 'If you love God, you will keep His commandments' (John 14:15). His commandment is that of love because He said, 'Thou shall love the Lord thy God... and thou shall love your neighbour as yourself' (Mark 12:30-31). It is upon the commandment of love that every other commandment is built. So, one of the ways you can prove that you love God is to love your neighbour also (John 14:15).

This kind of love cannot be engaged in the energy of the flesh. We need the help of the Holy Spirit to walk in the love that God has ordained for us. It is written,

> *And hope maketh not ashamed; because the love of God is shed abroad in our hearts by the Holy Ghost which is given unto us.*
>
> Romans 5:5

Also, it is written,

> *Love worketh no ill to his neighbour: therefore love is the fulfilling of the law.*
>
> Romans 13:10

Clearly, Christianity and our walk with God are love-based; so, every endeavour to please God should be centered on love. God showed us a perfect example by sacrificing His only begotten son Jesus, to redeem us from sin and the evils in the world.

One of the ways through which the Holy Spirit helps us to demonstrate love is by empowering us to **give**. You cannot love without giving and you cannot give willingly without love; both can only be done through the help of the Holy Spirit. The Bible records,

> *My little children, let us not love in word, neither in tongue; but in deed and in truth.*
>
> 1 John 3:18

It is very important to understand that giving is not limited to material things, though it includes that; much more, it is about the giving of yourself. We have read, seen and heard of people who selflessly gave themselves because of their love for God and His Kingdom. For instance, John G. Lake helped those with a deadly disease, Mother Theresa met the needs of orphans and the less privileged, Martin Luther King (Jnr) fought for equality of the blacks, and many others who have been selfless.

You can only be empowered by the Holy Ghost into this realm of love. May the grace to walk more in this realm of love become your portion henceforth!

He Teaches Us All Things

The Holy Spirit is the principal teacher in the journey of life. He does not only teach us, but also brings to our remembrance what we have been taught, when needed. Scripture says,

> **But the Comforter, which is the Holy Ghost, whom the Father will send in my name, he shall teach you all things, and bring all things to your remembrance, whatsoever I have said unto you.**
>
> John 14:26

Notably, what the Holy Spirit teaches does not only pertain to the Word, but everything you require to live a successful life. Amazingly, the Holy Spirit can teach you things about how to dress, talk, locate a place, manage your family, finance, etc.

There was a time in our ministry when we needed more land space for the ministry's work. My husband was on a trip and according to him, he was not praying about it at that time when the Holy Spirit told Him, 'Why ask Me for another land when you have not used up the one I gave you?' The Holy Spirit then instantly gave him practical steps on how to build and maximise the space the ministry had at the time. You might wonder, the Holy Spirit helping concerning buildings? Yes! He does! He is interested in every area of your life, if you let Him.

A brother once shared a testimony of how he was called in his company to help resolve an issue with a faulty equipment in their factory. Before then, so many experts had worked on it and even manufacturers had tried all they could but to no avail. When this brother was invited to check on the equipment, he said that he prayed for divine insight and the Holy Spirit told him, 'Check terminal 1, 2, 3'. As he obeyed, he discovered the fault and the equipment that had been faulty, with no solution from experts, began to work!

Right there, to them, he became a celebrity in his place of work!

The Holy Spirit is the master of knowledge! Wisdom and truth are in His custody and He is willing to reveal them to you if only you can trust His judgment and humbly ask for His help. It is written,

> *But the anointing which ye have received of him abideth in you, and ye need not that any man teach you: but as the same anointing teacheth you of all things, and is truth, and is no lie, and even as it hath taught you, ye shall abide in him.*
>
> 1 John 2:27

I vividly remember that many years ago, I learnt how to drive and obtained my driver's licence practically through the help of the Holy Spirit.

Do not limit the Holy Spirit! The deeper your relationship with Him, the more He reveals things to you and the more glorious your life becomes. It is recorded,

> *But we all, with open face beholding as in a glass the glory of the Lord, are changed into the same*

image from glory to glory, even as by the Spirit of the Lord.

2 Corinthians 3:18

Also, the Holy Spirit helps our daily conversations. James 3:2 says, **For in many things we offend all. If any man offend not in word, the same is a perfect man, and able also to bridle the whole body.** It is through the help of the Spirit that we will not offend in words, because He gives the wisdom to speak rightly. To be discreet in your conversations, you need the help of the Holy Spirit. It is written,

Let your speech be alway with grace, seasoned with salt, that ye may know how ye ought to answer every man.

Colossians 4:6

To achieve this, the Bible says,

For the Holy Ghost shall teach you in the same hour what ye ought to say.

Luke 12:12

Therefore, with the baptism of the Holy Spirit and constant refilling, it is my prayer that your ways and speech shall be more pleasing unto God!

He Brings All Things To Our Remembrance

The truth is: What we remember as well as the act of remembering itself requires help. Life is full of so many activities, which can make you forget what should be of priority to you. Joseph F. Smith said: 'The office and duty of the Holy Ghost is to bring to our remembrance things that are past, to make clear to our understanding things that are present, and to show us things that are to come'. It is written,

> *But the Comforter, which is the Holy Ghost, whom the Father will send in my name, he shall ... bring all things to your remembrance, whatsoever I have said unto you.*
>
> *John 14:26*

Remembrance has to do with recollecting what you knew, because it is impossible to remember what you don't know. Jesus said the Holy Spirit would bring to our remembrance all that He has said to us, and all He has said to us is in the Word. Therefore, the Holy Spirit reminds us of what the Word says concerning every issue that confronts us.

For instance, there may be times when the devil may want to remind you of your past errors to condemn you. At such times, the Holy Spirit brings to your remembrance God's Word concerning forgiveness and this brings a soothing relief to you (Romans 8:1). Also, when you are confronted with challenges, the Holy Spirit can bring to your remembrance relevant scriptures to handle such issues; and whenever you encounter revelation concerning any situation, and engage it, you become victorious. The Bible says,

> *Thy words were found, and I did eat them; and thy word was unto me the joy and rejoicing of mine heart: for I am called by thy name, O Lord God of hosts.*
>
> *Jeremiah 15:16*

The Holy Spirit can remind you of anything and everything, even the minutest details of an event. He is very detailed and there is no other person who can accurately remind you of anything, like Him.

There was a day I misplaced an item in my home and was searching for it. It suddenly occurred to me that I could engage the help of the Holy Spirit to get the job done. I instantly did and almost immediately, I was able to locate what I had been searching for.

To Protects Us From Wicked Forces

The Holy Spirit is a multifunctional personality. He is one Spirit, Who performs various functions depending on your knowledge of Him. He will only be to you what you allow Him to be and He will not force His ways on you.

One of His very vital functions is to protect us from all the devices, traps and fiery darts of the enemy. The devil comes in various ways and will attempt to attack any area of one's life – family, health, career, finance and even your spiritual life. But thank God, the Bible says,

...When the enemy shall come in like a flood, the Spirit of the LORD shall lift up a standard against him.

Isaiah 59:19

It is the Spirit of God that raises a standard against all the devices of the enemy that may want to victimise you. The Holy Spirit, like a mighty flood, sweeps off all the plans and attacks of the enemy against you. Remember, life is a battlefield and as a believer, you need the power of the Holy Spirit to overcome the wicked oppositions. The world is full of wickedness, but with God's power at work in you, you can triumph over the enemy (Psalm 74:20).

One of the ways the Holy Spirit protects us from wicked forces is through **the Word.** He gives us the right Word to deal with the devil and his agents. The devil will not bow to how fluent you speak, but how much of the Word of God you know. This Word is what is referred to as light. With the light of God's Word, you are sure to displace every darkness. The Bible says,

And the light shineth in darkness; and the darkness comprehended it not.

John 1:5

Therefore, when you have the right Word and the Word in season as given to you by the Holy Spirit, every opposition will bow to your authority over them.

He Empowers Our Worship Of God

'Worship' means total reverence for God; that is, loosening up yourself in complete adoration of God. This, you cannot do in the energy of the flesh. With the flesh, it is impossible to please God and the Bible says he that giveth thanks in the Spirit doeth it well (1 Corinthians 14:16-17). There is no way you can give quality worship to God without the help of the Holy Spirit, because He empowers our worship (1 Corinthians 14:15, 17).

Remember: The Holy Spirit helps us on the prayer altar, and worship is an integral part of prayer. So, the Holy Spirit enables us to give God what is due to Him, instead of murmuring and complaining. It is written,

> **God is a Spirit: and they that worship him must worship him in spirit and in truth.**
>
> *John 4:24*

Also, it is written,

> **...We are the circumcision, which worship God in the spirit, and rejoice in Christ Jesus, and have no confidence in the flesh.**
>
> *Philippians 3:3*

Worship is one thing that God cannot do for Himself. Therefore, when you worship God, you are doing for God what He cannot do for Himself. However, acceptable worship requires the help of the Holy Spirit.

The realm the Holy Spirit wants to bring you into is the realm where you are completely lost in God's presence. It is the realm where you do not need to ask for anything, but you are made whole in His presence. It is also that level where nothing around you makes meaning, just God! Therefore, today, seek to engage the Holy Spirit in a hearty session of worship and just enjoy the presence of God; then watch how He engages Himself mightily on your behalf!

He Sanctifies Us

The Holy Spirit is the Spirit of holiness and He is sent to purge the believer of every impurity, thereby making us fit for the Kingdom of God. Read this scripture carefully,

> *And such were some of you: but ye are washed, but ye are sanctified, but ye are justified in the name of the Lord Jesus, and by the Spirit of our God.*
>
> *1 Corinthians 6:11*

Without the sanctification mission of the Holy Spirit, we are not qualified to be called the children of God. We can only be called God's children when we are washed by the Spirit (Romans 8:14; 1 Corinthians 3:21).

To be sanctified means to be washed and purged of every form of filthiness that can disqualify us from God's Kingdom. Our God is holy and cannot behold iniquity; therefore, He through the Spirit, takes off that filth from us so we can approach Him with boldness.

In Acts 5, the sanctification ministry of the Holy Spirit to the church was demonstrated by dealing with Ananias and Sapphira. It is written,

> *And great fear came upon all the church, and upon as many as heard these things.*
>
> *Acts 5:11*

When you give the Holy Spirit a chance in your life, He enables you to live righteously; He searches you daily so your heart can always be right with God. Just as the Psalmist said,

> *Search me, O God, and know my heart: try me, and know my thoughts:*
>
> *And see if there be any wicked way in me, and lead me in the way everlasting.*
>
> *Psalm 139:23-24*

Just as is mine, your heart cry daily should be for the Holy Spirit to enable you live holy and blameless until the end. It is written,

> *That he might sanctify and cleanse it with the washing of water by the word,*
>
> *That he might present it to himself a glorious church, not having spot, or wrinkle, or any such thing; but that it should be holy and without blemish.*
>
> *Ephesians 5:26-27*

It is very important, therefore, that you *lift up the hands which hang down, and the feeble knees; and make straight paths for your feet, lest that which is lame be turned out of the way; but let it rather be healed* (Hebrews 12:12-13). My prayer for you is that you receive grace to constantly yield to the Holy Spirit and receive His help to enable you live a sanctified life till the end.

'Holiness, as taught in the Scriptures, is not based upon knowledge on our part. Rather, it is based upon the resurrected Christ in-dwelling us and changing us into His likeness'

– *A. W. Tozer*

The Holy Spirit: His Fruits

But the fruit of the Spirit is love, joy, peace, longsuffering, gentleness, goodness, faith,

Meekness, temperance: against such there is no law.

Galatians 5:22-23

It is interesting to know that the Holy Spirit is a fruit-bearing personality. The fruit of the Spirit represents the character expected of a believer and this is embedded in the Holy Spirit. Remember, we are the planting of the Lord and plants are expected to bear fruits. Just as a tree that bears mango fruit is called a mango tree, so a life that is evident with the fruit of the Spirit is said to be living by the Spirit. It is written,

...That they might be called trees of righteousness, the planting of the Lord, that he might be glorified.

Isaiah 61:3

When you allow God's Spirit to live in and through

you, the Spirit produces a set of Christ-like qualities or virtues within you, called the fruit of the Spirit. This fruit is manifested in our relationship with God and others, both believers and unbelievers.

Think of this: Naturally, a single fruit can give several vitamins, so it is with the Holy Spirit. This explains why the Bible says, *...But the fruit (not fruits) of the Spirit...* (Galatians 5:22). The fruit of the Holy Spirit is filled with various nutrients for our daily living; nine visible attributes expected of a true Christian life. This fruit according to Galatians 5:22-23 includes:

Love: We live in a world where the subject of love is often talked about, but rarely truly practiced. Sadly, many people tend to look for love in wrong places and most times, love is expressed in wrong ways. The love of the Holy Spirit comes from a regenerated spirit and it is characterised by a selfless attitude that gives freely, without demanding anything in return. God is love and we are begotten of Him through the love He has for us. Therefore, as a child born of love, you are expected to love as a proof that you possess the nature of your Father God. The Bible says,

> *Hereby perceive we the love of God, because he laid down his life for us: and we ought to lay down our lives for the brethren.*
>
> *1 John 3:16*

1 Corinthians 13 presents a full package of what the

fruit of love entails. This love is kind, does no evil, is not proud and not easily provoked. This kind of love does not seek to hurt and it does not take revenge when hurt. That is why the Bible calls love the fulfilling of the law (Romans 13:10). With God's definition of love, you will understand that it is impossible to love in the energy of the flesh. That is why love is a fruit of the Holy Spirit; you will require the help of the Holy Spirit to love the way God expects. It means that it is not something that is in the human nature, but one that is divine. It is written,

> *...The love of God is shed abroad in our hearts by the Holy Ghost which is given unto us.*
>
> *Romans 5:5*

The Holy Spirit spreads the all-surpassing love of God in our hearts. This kind of love emanates from the inside and cannot fail. First, you must love God. Without loving God, it will be impossible to love others because it is the love of God in you, as imputed by the Spirit, that radiates to those around you (Ephesians 3:17-19). Do you really love God? Think deeply about this!

Love is severally defined as the unselfish, loyal, self-denying, self-sacrificing, Christ-like and benevolent concern for the well-being of others. As humans, our ability to love to this extent is very limited. This is why it is important for us to walk closely with the Holy Spirit to get this fruit working in us because it is impossible to truly walk in love without the help of the Holy Spirit.

Joy: The infilling of the Holy Spirit comes with an overflowing joy from within. This type of joy has nothing to do with the circumstances around you because it is a Spirit-given expression that flourishes at all times, even in unpleasant situations. The Bible says,

> *...For the joy of the Lord is your strength.*
> *Nehemiah 8:10*

Notably, the fruit of joy thrives on our relationship with God. Living a joyful life shows that you have understanding of God's plan for your life. It was said of Jesus, *...Who for the joy that was set before Him endured the cross, despising the shame, and is set down at the right hand of the throne of God* (Hebrews 12:2). Beyond all that was happening around Him and the suffering on the cross, Jesus could see the glorious future that God had in store for Him. That is the kind of joy God wants you to possess; the joy that sees beyond the present. As it is written,

> *For the kingdom of God is not meat and drink; but righteousness, and peace, and joy in the Holy Ghost.*
> *Romans 14:17*

Joy is an evidence of the presence of God in your life. If you are endued with the person of the Holy Spirit, this fruit of the Spirit will be obvious in your life. The fruit of joy is not a temporal feeling of satisfaction, but a divine empowerment to be joyful always (Philippians 4:4). My uttermost desire and prayer for you as you read this today is that your joy, no man shall take from you!

Peace: The Old Testament word for 'peace' is the same as the Hebrew word called 'shalom'. This means 'wholeness'. The New Testament Greek word for peace is 'eirene', which is translated as oneness, quietness or rest.

Peace is a state of calmness that emanates from a desperate desire for God. Clearly, without God, it is impossible to experience true peace. Daily events in the media, characterised by diverse news of chaos, terrorist attacks, famines and other evil occurrences, seek to take away peace. However, when the fruit of peace that surpasses all understanding comes on you, you remain at rest, the happenings around notwithstanding. A person of peace is calm, has inner strength that results in the ability to be composed in the midst of trying circumstances. It is written,

> *Peace I leave with you, my peace I give unto you: not as the world giveth, give I unto you. Let not your heart be troubled, neither let it be afraid.*
> John 14:27

A wise man once said, 'Peace is not the absence of conflict, but the presence of God no matter the conflict'. The Holy Spirit gives peace no matter the prevailing circumstances. Personally, I have always enjoyed God's peace, even when things seem not to be as expected. It is real! I am a beneficiary! Scripture says,

> *And let the peace of God rule in your hearts, to the which also ye are called in one body; and be ye thankful.*
>
> *Colossians 3:15*

To the glory of God, my home is a faith-filled home and you cannot exercise faith without the peace of God. This peace is expressed and grows through a constant walk with the Holy Spirit, who is the embodiment of peace.

In this embattled world, may you begin to enjoy more of this kind of peace than ever!

Longsuffering: This means to be patient, forbearing, enduring, etc. You will agree with me that to exercise these, require grace. The Bible says,

> *Strengthened with all might, according to his glorious power, unto all patience and longsuffering with joyfulness;*
>
> *Colossians 1:11*

It is clear that you cannot be patient or forbear without the help of the Holy Spirit. Daily, you are confronted with issues that require you to flare-up or react, but the Holy Spirit enables you to keep calm at all times. Indeed, there is need for patience in our Christian walk, because it is through patience that we can obtain God's promises. It is written,

For ye have need of patience, that, after ye have done the will of God, ye might receive the promise.
Hebrews 10:36

This is truly a virtue – something rare but valuable. It is rare because not many people possess it and valuable because it is priceless. Indeed, there is no one who truly possess the virtue of patience that is not highly esteemed (Hebrews 6:12).

As for me, I hunger and thirst for more of this now than ever. I pray this will be your desire as well!

Gentleness: The presence of the Holy Spirit in you makes you kind and tender-hearted. Someone who is kind is usually nice. To 'be nice' is to be friendly or polite, but the fruit of gentleness goes beyond that. It entails acting for the good of people regardless of what they do. It is having a heart of service that goes beyond rewards. It is written,

Now I Paul myself beseech you by the meekness and gentleness of Christ, who in presence am base among you, but being absent am bold toward you:
2 Corinthians 10:1

When you possess the fruit of gentleness, you will correct others with simplicity, understanding and love, instead of being hurt, resentful and angry. You will speak with calmness and humbleness of heart, regardless of who the person is or what they have done. You will not behave unruly even when people are not around. Gentleness has nothing to do with whether you speak loudly or not; it has to do with your character – the way you present yourself and your words. This is majorly tested when you are not watchful, which is usually when out of the view of familiar faces. Apostle Paul in his letter to the church in Ephesus said,

> *I therefore, the prisoner of the Lord, beseech you that ye walk worthy of the vocation wherewith ye are called,*
>
> *With all lowliness and meekness, with longsuffering, forbearing one another in love;*
>
> *Endeavouring to keep the unity of the Spirit in the bond of peace.*
>
> *Ephesians 4:1-3*

May the fruit of gentleness begin to find expression in your life in a greater dimension than ever!

Goodness: The Holy Spirit empowers us to do good at all times. Humanly speaking, it is impossible to be good at all times, because the human nature is characterised by sin. The Bible says that the heart of man is deep and desperately wicked (Jeremiah 17:9). It is the presence of God in you that turns this wickedness to goodness. The Bible says,

> *For it is God which worketh in you both to will and to do of his good pleasure.*
>
> *Philippians 2:13*

When you are good, you please God who is always good, no matter the circumstance (Acts 10:38). God's goodness has nothing to do with you being righteous or not. For example, God makes the sun to shine both on the good and the evil (Mathew 5:45). That is how good God is! The seed of goodness that the Holy Spirit gives has no respect for persons or circumstances. He gives you the grace if you will, to act out His nature at all times. As it is written,

> *But to do good and to communicate forget not: for with such sacrifices God is well pleased.*
>
> Hebrews 13:16

Receive that grace now, in Jesus name!

Faith: The kind of faith referred to here is different from the Spirit of faith and the gift of faith. Some translations, other than King James, refer to it as faithfulness. That is, the act of trusting and being committed to God. It is what gives you an assurance at new birth that you are a child of God. The Holy Spirit deposits in you the heart to trust God and be loyal to Him (Romans 10:9-10). Scripture says,

> *Now the God of hope fill you with all joy and peace in believing, that ye may abound in hope, through the power of the Holy Ghost.*
>
> Romans 15:13

Faith is believing that God is who He says He is and

continuing in that belief despite the complexities of life. I encourage you to trust God that He will work His will in you, and whatever good happens today is nothing compared to your future reward in heaven. However, the only way to have such faith is by the Holy Spirit's influence; He testifies of the truth and propels us to seek God (Romans 8:16).

Meekness: This is characterised by quietness, gentility and an attitude of submission. The fruit of meekness keeps you humble, no matter the height you attain. It makes you realise that all that you are and have is given to you by God and that whatever He has blessed you with is purely by grace. It is written,

> *But the meek shall inherit the earth; and shall delight themselves in the abundance of peace.*
> *Psalm 37:11*

John Riskin said: 'I believe the first test of a truly great man is his humility. I do not mean by humility, doubt of his own power, or hesitation in speaking his opinion. But really great men have a ...feeling that the greatness is not in them but through them; that they could not do or be anything else than God made them'. I want you to meditate deeply on that!

Exhibiting the fruit of meekness shows your level of spiritual maturity and James 3:13 says, *Who is a wise man and endued with knowledge among you?*

let him shew out of a good conversation his works with meekness of wisdom. Primarily, a meek person is one who is willing to totally surrender to the control of the Spirit and I have established the fact that one of the missions of the Holy Spirit is to lead you through the journey of life. But, without the virtue of meekness, you cannot be led by the Holy Spirit (Psalm 25:9).

Therefore, to be constantly led by the Holy Spirit, which culminates in your being endued with power, the fruit of meekness is non-negotiable, as only then can you receive God's eternal promise (Matthew 5:5).

Temperance: This is also called self-control. It means saying 'no' to yourself in times of ungodly desires, and doing what is right or what needs to be done, per time. This virtue is necessary to overcome the desires of the flesh. There is constant war between obeying the flesh and the spirit. Man is triune in nature; he is a spirit that lives in a body and has a soul. Most times, the soul is torn between submitting either to the will of the flesh or to the spirit. This is where self-control or temperance comes in.

To live by the Spirit, you must walk in the Spirit and when you walk in the Spirit, you will not fulfil the lusts of the flesh (Galatians 5:16, 25). Therefore, the Spirit helps to curb every fleshly desire that may spring up from within. Apostle Paul said,

But I keep under my body, and bring it into subjection: lest that by any means, when I have preached to others, I myself should be a castaway.

1 Corinthians 9:27

Doubtless, the Holy Spirit helps you keep a balanced behaviour at all times. He keeps you calm in times of adversities and helps you withstand temptations because He is the Spirit of sanctification. He also reproves you of every wrong done, empowers your tongue and refrains you from speaking evil.

The fruit of the Spirit is a virtue all believers should possess, because it differentiates you as a child of God, from the world. It is written,

In this the children of God are manifest, and the children of the devil: whosoever doeth not righteousness is not of God, neither he that loveth not his brother.

1 John 3:10

You must consciously strive to see these virtues manifest in your life in a growing dimension. Indeed, there is a race to be run and a heaven to make. You shall make it! The Word of God says,

Whereby are given unto us exceeding great and precious promises: that by these ye might be partakers of the divine nature, having escaped the corruption that is in the world through lust.

And beside this, giving all diligence, add to your

faith virtue; and to virtue knowledge;

And to knowledge temperance; and to temperance patience; and to patience godliness;

And to godliness brotherly kindness; and to brotherly kindness charity.

2 Peter 1:4-7

The fruit of the Spirit is what every believer cannot do without because it is required for our daily walk with God. To live a triumphant Christian life, possessing the fruit of the Spirit is non-negotiable; it enables you to walk according to the Spirit, thus reflecting on your daily activities. In the words of Jonathan Edwards, 'The Spirit of God is given to the true saints to dwell in them as His proper lasting abode, to dwell in them and to influence their hearts as a principle of new nature or as a divine supernatural spring of life and action'.

In a world filled with men of charisma but no character, it is critically important for you to seek to manifest the fruit of the Spirit in a growing dimension in your life because it is the hallmark of true Christianity!

'It is deeply important that the believer's mind be renewed after the image of Jesus. That's one reason He sent the Holy Ghost to indwell us and be our Teacher and Guide'

– Kenneth E. Hagin

The Holy Spirit: His Gifts

Now there are diversities of gifts, but the same Spirit.

And there are differences of administrations, but the same Lord.

And there are diversities of operations, but it is the same God which worketh all in all.

1 Corinthians 12:4-6

Spiritual gifts, as the gifts of the Holy Spirit are often called, are weapons in the hands of the believer to help us minister the love, life and power of Jesus Christ through the supernatural, miraculous manifestations direct from the Holy Spirit Himself. These gifts, embedded in the Holy Ghost for our profiting, are available to every believer for the edification of the church; that is, building up of others to the glory of God and to fortify us as individuals. The gifts also help to equip us to find fulfilment in the area of our God-given assignment or ministry, as the central thrust of your God-given assignment depends on the spiritual gifts you have received. Sadly, often times, we neglect them to our loss.

Although, the gifts differ in operation, they are all activated and bestowed on us from one source, which is the Holy Ghost, as an act of divine grace, rather than by natural ability, and He gives to everyone as He pleases. As the scriptures says, ***But all these worketh that one and the selfsame Spirit, dividing to every man severally as he will*** (1 Corinthians 12:11).

Think on this: In the words of Donald Bloesch, 'A church where Charismatic gifts in all their wonder and variety are not in evidence is something less than the Church founded at Pentecost'. The Bible says,

> ***For the kingdom of God is not in word, but in power.***
>
> *1 Corinthians 4:20*

In Ephesians 4:11-12, the various ministries in the church are listed and you can always find your calling or assignment in one or more of these offices because ***He gave some, apostles; and some, prophets; and some, evangelists; and some, pastors and teachers; for the perfecting of the saints, for the work of the ministry, for the edifying of the body of Christ.***

Please understand: One of the most important steps to flowing in the gifts of the Holy Spirit is to earnestly desire them. The Holy Spirit is the custodian of divine secrets and He reveals them to whom He wills, but you have to desire it. This explains why the Bible admonishes us to covet earnestly the best gifts. As it is written,

> **But the manifestation of the Spirit is given to every man to profit withal.**
>
> **But covet earnestly the best gifts...**
>
> *1 Corinthians 12:7, 31*

Jesus, in His earthly ministry, as well as the disciples after being endued with power, used these gifts effectively to validate the accuracy of their message. It is written,

> **How shall we escape, if we neglect so great salvation; which at the first began to be spoken by the Lord, and was confirmed unto us by them that heard him;**
> **God also bearing them witness, both with signs and wonders, and with divers miracles, <u>and gifts of the Holy Ghost</u>, according to his own will?**
>
> *Hebrews 2:3-4 (Emphasis mine)*

I strongly believe that one of the reasons the body of Christ is not making greater impact today, in our generation, is because of our failure to operate in the gifts of the Holy Spirit as the early Disciples and Missionaries did.

Notably, most of the preaching done today in the name of the Lord is without the power of the Holy Spirit, manifesting through the gifts of the Spirit. I am sure that greater multitudes will be cheaply won by the saving grace of our Lord Jesus Christ and delivered from the power of darkness by the demonstration of God's power, through the manifestations of the gifts of the Holy Spirit.

Jesus and the early Apostles had their sermons validated by the presence of the supernatural. We should not do any less! Christianity without the supernatural is superficial. Jesus said, *If I do not the works of my Father, believe me not* (John 10:37).

These gifts are for the edification of the body of Christ and all you need to do is to earnestly desire to have them. Just imagine how many people can be saved, healed, delivered and helped out of their negative situations, if you will allow the Holy Spirit to manifest some of these gifts through you from time to time. Hear this: You are carrying somebody's miracle; learn and desire to let the gifts flow!

Classification of the Gifts of the Spirit

For to one is given by the Spirit the word of wisdom; to another the word of knowledge by the same Spirit;

To another faith by the same Spirit; to another the gifts of healing by the same Spirit;

To another the working of miracles; to another prophecy; to another discerning of spirits; to another divers kinds of tongues; to another the interpretation of tongues:

1 Corinthians 12:8-10

Interestingly, the gifts of the Spirit are nine in number and no two gifts are the same and generally, no two believers have exactly the same gifts. However, these gifts are given for the benefit of the church. The nine gifts can be easily classified into three according to their operations. These include:

Revelation Gifts

These include the word of wisdom, word of knowledge and discerning of spirits.

As the name implies, it has to do with unveiling or making known publicly what has been kept secret. The gifts of revelation are of the core ministries of the Holy Spirit, because when He was introduced to the church, it was said of Him that He will reveal to us all things as He hears from the Father (John 14:26, 16:14).

Also, it is written that unto us it is given to know the mysteries of the Kingdom (Mark 4:11). Therefore, the gift of revelation has been given to the believer to know God's plans for now and the future, and to be able to discern between His will and that of the enemy. These gifts of revelation according to 1 Corinthians 12:8 include word of wisdom, word of knowledge and discerning of spirits; and they all work interactively one with another. In the words of John Rea, author of *The Layman's Commentary on the Holy Spirit*, these gifts have been 'given to Christians to enable them to know what to do or say in specific situations'.

The Word of Wisdom

This is God revealing His mind, purpose and plan to an individual; it has nothing to do with the world's view of wisdom. It is a supernatural perspective to ascertain the divine means for accomplishing God's will in a given situation. It is also a divinely given power to appropriate spiritual intuition in solving problems. It is speaking hidden truths of what is not known; it tells you of things to come or how to handle things in the future. It is different from the word of knowledge which will be discussed later. It is received from God mainly through prayers (Ephesians 1:17).

In the New Testament, there are two occasions when one of the Prophets, Agabus, flowing in the word of wisdom spoke about what was to happen, in order to prepare the people for things that were ahead.

Read this account carefully,

> **And there stood up one of them named Agabus, and signified by the spirit that there should be great dearth throughout all the world: which came to pass in the days of Claudius Caesar.**
>
> *Acts 11:28*

Also, in Acts 21:10-11, the Bible records,

> *And as we tarried there many days, there came down from Judaea a certain prophet, named Agabus.*
>
> *And when he was come unto us, he took Paul's girdle, and bound his own hands and feet, and said, Thus saith the Holy Ghost, So shall the Jews at Jerusalem bind the man that owneth this girdle, and shall deliver him into the hands of the Gentiles*

It is evident from the above scriptures that Agabus was neither prophesying about doctrines nor giving Paul guidance or direction but was merely telling Paul what awaited him in Jerusalem.

The word of wisdom is a gift which cannot be gained through study or experience and should by no means try to replace them. It is the supernatural impartation of facts. The wisdom of God is the Word of God and you cannot walk in this wisdom without the fear of God, which is the beginning of all wisdom (Proverbs 1:7).

It is written,

> *For to one is given by the Spirit the word of wisdom...*
> *1 Corinthians 12:8*

Jesus, throughout His ministry, operated in the fullness of this gift; He was able to know God's plan for every moment by the prompting of the Spirit. He made statements such as 'It is not the will of the Father' or 'My time has not yet come'. That was because He knew

God's will and plan per time. For example, He said to the Samaritan woman, **'The hour cometh...'** (John 4:23). That is unveiling what will happen in the future.

The word of wisdom has to do with a revelation of what God will do. God reveals His plans to believers, because the mysteries of the Kingdom are for those who are in the Kingdom. What are mysteries? Mysteries are divine secrets and it is the unveiling of these secrets to an individual that is called the gift of the word of wisdom (Mark 4:11). It is written,

> *The secret of the Lord is with them that fear him;*
> *and he will shew them his covenant.*
>
> *Psalm 25:14*

By one word of wisdom, **Daniel** was able to see what would happen in generations to come (Daniel 9:1). In the same vein, a person who is said to operate in this gift can through the inspiration of the Holy Spirit say what would happen next in a particular situation. It is not intuition, but a vivid account as unveiled by God.

It is called a word, because it comes in seasons as prompted by the Spirit. It is not a vision or dream, but can come through that medium. For instance, **Joseph** received a word of wisdom when God revealed to him what the future holds as recorded in Genesis 37:5-7. This came into manifestation just as he said it.

Many prophets of old such as **Jeremiah**, **Isaiah**,

Amos, **Zechariah**, etc., manifested this gift. If we must know and fulfil God's plan for us, then we should covet earnestly this gift.

Precisely on April 10, 1982, God revealed to His servant, Dr. David Oyedepo, how he would be ministering in a place and millions of people would be listening to him at the same time. This was at a time when the internet was not in view. Today, millions of people across the globe listen to God's Word through His servant, by connecting online, just as God said it!

Truly, God will not perform anything on the earth without revealing it first to His servants. Think on these: When God was to destroy the world with a flood, He told **Noah** about it (Genesis 6:13-17). When He was to destroy Sodom and Gomorrah, **Abraham** was informed (Genesis 18:17). Before Jesus came into the world, several prophets including prophet **Isaiah** spoke of His coming (Isaiah 9:6). Even the manifestation of the Holy Spirit was revealed long before He came to stay on the earth (Joel 2:28; Isaiah 28:11).

The word of wisdom can also be given to Christians to enable them know what to do or say in specific situations. In some difficult or dangerous situations, a word of wisdom may be given which would resolve the difficulty or silence the opponent. For instance, when the Pharisees tried to trap Jesus with their question about paying tax to Caesar, He manifested in the gift of the word of wisdom by saying, *Render therefore unto Caesar the things which are Caesar's; and unto God the things that are God's* (Matthew 22:21).

The first test **Solomon** encountered as soon as God gave him *a wise and an understanding heart* (1 Kings 3:12) was that of two harlots claiming ownership of a child. His word of wisdom calling for a sword to divide the baby into two, revealed the true mother of the child (1 Kings 3:16-28).

God has promised us similar wisdom in needed times, if we will earnestly crave its manifestation in any difficult situation, *For the Holy Ghost shall teach you in the same hour what ye ought to say* (Luke 12:12).

This gift is God's revelation to man and it is still operational today, but the Holy Spirit gives it as He wills. The good news is: As you learn to yield to God, He will reveal His plans to you by His Spirit.

The Word of Knowledge

The word of knowledge is the supernatural insight or understanding of circumstances, situations, problems or facts by revelation solely by divine aid. It can be regarded as a supernatural revelation of facts – past, present or future, not naturally learned. A manifestation of the word of knowledge is required when information is needed immediately and the only way to get it is through supernatural means. In 1 Corinthians 2:16, it is written, ...*we have the mind of Christ.*

This gift of the Holy Spirit, I believe, will manifest with a lot of frequency in your daily life with the Lord, if you can learn how to get it from Him as He releases it. Since our level of knowledge as humans is imperfect, incomplete and very limited, it is wisdom, then, that we frequently receive words of knowledge from God, who has perfect knowledge of all things. This will enable us to go through life successfully, protect us from being harmed and help to fulfil our God-ordained destinies.

I believe that the Holy Spirit actually manifests this gift a lot more than believers realise. However, many fail to either realise it or pick it up when it comes their way, probably because they have never been taught that the Holy Spirit can do this for them in the first place.

Really, the word of knowledge that you can receive directly from the Holy Spirit can literally cover an infinite number of things in your daily life. They can cover anything from something very trivial such as where you may have misplaced your car keys, to giving you life-saving knowledge on how to prevent an impending crisis or emergency. This gift is also very important because it shows us how to pray more effectively and/or reveals exactly the kind of help a person needs in prayer.

The gifts of the word of wisdom and the word of knowledge function together; knowledge is a raw material and wisdom builds on it. While the word of wisdom is futuristic, the word of knowledge is God's revelation of what will happen at the instance or what has already happened. It is simply the Holy Spirit transmitting His specific knowledge to you on something that you have no ability or means to know about with your limited intelligence and knowledge level. For instance, Peter said to Ananias and Sapphira by the gift of the word of knowledge,

> *...Ananias, why hath Satan filled thine heart to lie to the Holy Ghost, and to keep back part of the price of the land?*
>
> *Whiles it remained, was it not thine own? and after it was sold, was it not in thine own power? why hast thou conceived this thing in thine heart? thou hast not lied unto men, but unto God...*
>
> *Then Peter said unto her, How is it that ye have agreed together to tempt the Spirit of the Lord? behold, the feet of them which have buried thy husband are at the door, and shall carry thee out.*
>
> *Acts 5:3-4, 9*

This is a practical example of the Holy Spirit revealing to someone what has happened. Also, reading through the miracles of Jesus and the Apostles, one will find the phrase 'perceiving that he has faith'; this means, 'knowing that he has faith'. The word of knowledge is a knowing; it is receiving information from the Holy Spirit. It is written,

But God hath revealed them unto us by his Spirit: for the Spirit searcheth all things, yea, the deep things of God.

For what man knoweth the things of a man, save the spirit of man which is in him? even so the things of God knoweth no man, but the Spirit of God.

Now we have received, not the spirit of the world, but the spirit which is of God; that we might know the things that are freely given to us of God.

1 Corinthians 2:10-12

Acts 10 clearly shows two perspectives in which the Holy Spirit gives a word of knowledge. His mission to the Gentiles was revealed to Peter in a **vision**, and He also told him **verbally** that some people were there to see him. Isn't this amazing?

How then, exactly, does the Holy Spirit transmit an actual word of knowledge to us? I believe the number one way that He will communicate a word of knowledge to us is through the inner knowing. The Bible says that the Holy Spirit bears 'witness' with our human spirits (Romans 8:16).

This inner witness is what I call the inner knowing. Suddenly, you will receive a 'without-a-doubt' type of knowing on the information that He is transmitting to you. It comes as a definite conviction, in form of a vision or by a scripture that is quickened into your spirit. Furthermore, it can be revealed as a thought, an impression on your mind or a knowing that comes to you in a similitude (a mental picture in your mind's eye). These pictures can be used to give you quite a bit of information and insight on what He is trying to give you knowledge on.

The only issue with such pictures in your mind's eye is that you have to learn how to discern the difference between a vision from the Holy Spirit and that of your own natural imagination. This is because your natural imagination has the power and ability to make up its own mental pictures in your mind's eye.

For example, when at the onset of this ministry, my husband, Dr. David Oyedepo, thought that the base of this ministry would be in Jos, Northern Nigeria, at the commissioning, prayer was said over the city of Jos and even an advance party of staff were sent ahead. After the commissioning service, when my husband took time to give thanks to God about the upcoming start in Jos, suddenly, God told him that He was not the One sending him to Jos. He then reminded my husband of a time when he was playing table tennis in Jos and said in his heart that if he was opportune in the future, he would want to live there. God told him that was what he had heard, not Him. God then instructed him to stay back in the city we were, which he did. Later, God led him to move to Kaduna in Northern Nigeria, and he obeyed. I can't imagine what would have become of this ministry operating out of God's will, had he not had that encounter!

As you can see from these examples, there is literally nothing that the Holy Spirit cannot be involved in, regarding your personal life. He can give you a word of knowledge on how to properly handle something that you are currently dealing with or to help others with their situations.

Think of the dimensions and possibilities with just this one special gift alone – the supernatural knowledge and insight being given directly to you by the Holy Spirit, not by your own mind or intelligence. That is, the Holy Spirit Himself transmitting His own divine knowledge to you on something that you cannot solve or figure out on your own. Apostle Paul spoke extensively about this in 1 Corinthians 2.

Remember, one of the missions of the Holy Spirit is to make life comfortable for the believer. What better way to do this than to reveal to you every step of your journey through life? The Holy Spirit, through the word of knowledge, will reveal your errors, grant you a way of escape, give instructions and directions, etc. The Bible clearly states that without knowledge, one can be destroyed or held captive (Hosea 4:6).

The Discerning of Spirits

It is written,

But the manifestation of the Spirit is given to every

> *man to profit withal.*
>
> *For to one is given by the Spirit the word of wisdom;*
> *... to another discerning of <u>spirits;</u>*
>
> 1 Corinthians 12:7-8, 10

Note that the small letter 's' and the plural nature of spirits is a clear indication that it is not the Holy Spirit that is referred to in the above scripture. Rather, this scripture is referring to demonic spirits, God's angels and the human spirit.

In these very dangerous and perilous times that we live in today, I strongly believe that this is a gift everyone should covet earnestly. The *devil ... knoweth that he hath but a short time* (Revelation 12:12); so, he is doing more wickedly. His key tool which is deception will become the hallmark of these extremely dangerous times.

Simply, 'to discern' means to see, perceive or understand something that is not naturally clear. In this case, it is to perceive or understand the different spirits in operation in any given situation. It is a supernatural ability enabled by the Holy Spirit that allows a person to determine the source of a spiritual manifestation, whether it emanates from God, the devil or man. Clearly, everything we see physically is controlled in the spiritual and if we have this gift, God can reveal information about the presence or absence of spiritual entities.

Discerning of spirits gives supernatural insight into the spirit realm. This gift helps to discern the good and bad or evil spirit as well differentiate between the Spirit of truth from the spirit of error. With this gift, you can differentiate realities from counterfeits, the divine from the demonic, true teaching from false teaching and in some cases, spiritual from carnal motives. Usually, people regard this gift as useful to detect evil spiritual forces or influences. It can also detect the presence or absence of angelic intervention or the promptings of God's Holy Spirit working within us.

Clearly, we need this gift to be fully operational in our lives today, especially in our relationships with others. With the devil constantly appearing as an angel of light, you need the supernatural discerning insight and knowledge given by the Holy Spirit to know and fully expose the kind of spirit operating in anyone you are relating with.

At this point, I will briefly discuss the three types of spirits referred to in 1 Corinthians 12:10, and how you can identify their operations.

A. **Demonic Spirits:** With demonic spirits still roaming the earth today, demons can literally enter into a person's body, if they have the legal right to do so. Once they gain access, they hide very well, quietly operating through that person. You need this gift activated in you to be able to detect and expose such demons.

With the gift of discerning of spirits, you can

sometimes literally 'see' the demon manifest through the person's eyes. With eyes looking directly at you, you can see hate and evil staring from the person's eyes. You need this gift of discerning of spirits from the Holy Spirit to be able to see this when it happens.

Another way you can discern and sense demons in someone is through either a sense of smell or feeling. Some people will get a sick feeling in their stomach, like they want to vomit when they either see or get around someone who has a demon inside him.

Yet another way, which is most common, is through a strong inner knowing or a strong sensing from the Holy Spirit. You may not be able to feel, smell or see them in the person's eyes, but you can get a strong inner knowing or a strong conviction from the Holy Spirit that a particular person has demons inside him. A genuine and sincere walk with God and the Holy Spirit is required for you to operate with this gift at this level.

Oh, how every family needs this gift at work to save them from unnecessary heartaches! With this gift, you should be able to discern the spirit at work in anyone you bring into your home, particularly helpers in whose care you leave your children and wards. With spiritual sensitivity, you should sense when someone or something is not right.

For instance, there is a spirit behind every sickness or oppression and until you know that, you might not be able to overcome them effectively. Jesus, at some point, when healing the sick, made statements such as 'deaf and dumb spirit', 'spirit of infirmity', etc. He was addressing the spirit at work, because He could discern spirits. Some people come into homes and then, sicknesses and diseases begin to find expression. Their previously healthy children suddenly go in and out of hospitals as if it is normal. No! There is someone with a wrong spirit around you.

In Acts 16:16-18, Paul and Silas indeed cast out the spirit of divination from a damsel,

> *And it came to pass, as we went to prayer, a certain damsel possessed with a spirit of divination met us, which brought her masters much gain by soothsaying:*
>
> *The same followed Paul and us, and cried, saying, These men are the servants of the most high God, which shew unto us the way of salvation.*
>
> *And this did she many days. But Paul, being grieved, turned and said to the spirit, I command thee in the name of Jesus Christ to come out of her. And he came out the same hour.*

What the damsel was saying was true, but with a negative motive. Watch out for such people around you. They may be saying things that are true but their real motive is to get you to trust them enough and be comfortable around them, so as to give such people the opportunity for their manipulations and manifestations.

Please beware: The realm of the spirit is very real, although we cannot see it with our physical eyes. God has provided the gift of discerning of spirits to give the church supernatural insight into this spiritual realm and to ward off every evil.

The best safeguard to determine the authenticity of spiritual entities is God's Word, the Bible. To correctly examine a counterfeit currency bill, we have to know what a true currency bill looks like. God's Word resembles a crystal glass; this is because all the impurities have been purged out of it.

If we constantly practice, study and meditate on the teachings, instructions and guidance of the Bible, we will be able to detect whatever is not in harmony with the scriptures.

B. God's Angels: The Bible clearly states that God's angels are also spirit beings; they are ministering spirits. It is written,

But to which of the angels said he at any time, Sit on my right hand, until I make thine enemies thy footstool?

Are they not all ministering spirits, sent forth to minister for them who shall be heirs of salvation?

Hebrews 1:13-14

Throughout history, God's angels have appeared to people severally. The Bible is filled with these kinds of accounts from Daniel (Daniel 10:16-21) to Zachariah (Luke 1:11-19), to the Virgin Mary (Luke 1:28-38) and Apostle John in the book of Revelation (Revelation 1:1). However, the Bible also warns us that satan and his demons can appear to us as angels of light (2 Corinthians 11:14). As a result, you will need discernment from the Holy Spirit, if an angel were to ever appear to you. Even the Bible instructs,

> *Prove all things; hold fast that which is good.*
>
> *1 Thessalonians 5:21*

If an angel were to ever appear to you, the first thing you need to do is to properly test it. It is written,

> *Beloved, believe not every spirit, but try the spirits whether they are of God: because many false prophets are gone out into the world.*
>
> *Hereby know ye the Spirit of God: Every spirit that confesseth that Jesus Christ is come in the flesh is of God:*
>
> *1 John 4:1-2*

Ask the angel to identify who his Lord and Master is, and ask him to confess to you that Jesus Christ has come to our earth in the flesh. If he cannot make this direct confession to you, then you may be dealing with a demonic spirit disguising as an angel of light. Authoritatively command the demon to leave, in the name of Jesus Christ!

In addition to the above test, you could also receive

a strong discerning of spirits directly from the Holy Spirit. You will immediately sense that something is not right with that spirit and you will be able to pick it with a strong inner knowing that he is not from God. If he is an angel of God, you should feel a deep sense of peace and comfort coming from the Holy Spirit, as He should be bearing witness that this is one of God's angels.

In Matthew 24:4-5, the Bible records,

> **And Jesus answered and said unto them, Take heed that no man deceive you.**
>
> **For many shall come in my name, saying, I am Christ; and shall deceive many.**

From the above scripture, we can deduce from Jesus' warning that false 'Christian' ministers and ministries will have the capability to deceive many people by performing convincing, lying wonders and signs. These false ministers will demonstrate power – evil power – for the specific purpose of leading people astray, including some sincere believers. False prophets are known by their fruit – their conduct and actions (Matthew 7:15-20).

We have a clear warning from Apostle Paul that the battles we are confronted with daily cannot be won by conventional weapons that we can acquire from the world. The weapons we must seek should be spiritual, having the power to destroy arguments and every false claim that sets itself up against the knowledge of God and His Word (2 Corinthians 10:3-5). Therefore, always examine what a person or so-called prophet says to you, whether it agrees with the truth of God's Word or not.

C. **Human Spirits:** In addition to angels and demonic spirits, the third kind of spirit this gift is referring to is our own human spirits. For instance, someone could have a spirit of pride.

Definitely, a demonic spirit will not fill a person with pride; rather, it will be his own natural spirit, as we are all capable of being affected, especially in these last days when all manner of vices will be seeking to find expression in the lives of many. It is written,

> *This know also, that in the last days perilous times shall come.*
>
> *For men shall be lovers of their own selves, covetous, boasters, proud, blasphemers, disobedient to parents, unthankful, unholy,*
>
> *Without natural affection, trucebreakers, false accusers, incontinent, fierce, despisers of those that are good,*
>
> *Traitors, heady, highminded, lovers of pleasures more than lovers of God;*
>
> *Having a form of godliness, but denying the power thereof: from such turn away.*

For of this sort are they which creep into houses, and lead captive silly women laden with sins, led away with divers lusts,

2 Timothy 3:1-6

This gift will really be effective in discerning evil people; criminals such as rapists, money scammers and swindlers, fraudulent people and paedophiles who want to come around you and/or your family. A paedophile is a person who has sexual interest in children. Sadly, this is a growing challenge today, globally. Paedophiles are especially good at seducing some family members so they can work themselves into getting closer to some of their younger children. That is why parents especially have to keep a watchful eye on any new person who comes into their homes or immediate circle of family friends.

Realise that this is a gift that the Holy Spirit can manifest to you. Just be open and sensitive to anything that the Holy Spirit may want to transmit to you, if you ever encounter such evil people.

The good news is: God the Father is very protective of His own and will not hesitate to have His Holy Spirit give you major warning signals, if you ever cross paths with an evil person either targeting you, any of your close friends or family members for evil. Therefore, there is no reason to fear!

The Holy Spirit: His Gifts II

The Power Gifts

The gifts in this category are action gifts and they function on behalf of the believer to perform something impossible by ordinary human efforts. God intervenes with His sovereignty and glory to work this miracle.

Simply put, these are the creational gifts of the Holy Spirit. They involve doing something, putting things in place and performing what God has revealed. While the revelation gifts deal with God's plan for the present and the future, the power gifts bring those plans to fulfilment. According to 1 Corinthians 12:9-10, they include the following:

The Gift of Faith

It is written,

> *To another faith by the same Spirit...*
>
> 1 Corinthians 12:9

Clearly, there are different types of faith referred to in scriptures. The first kind of faith is **the saving faith**, which every believer who is born again has. This is the faith you are saved by and it comes by hearing and hearing by the Word of God (Romans 10:17). That faith believes the promises of God that if we confess our sins and believe in the Lord Jesus Christ, we shall be reconciled back to God by being born again. It is that faith in Jesus Christ as our Saviour that brings us salvation and makes us sons of God. As it is written,

> *But as many as received him, to them gave he power to become the sons of God, even to them that believe on his name.*
>
> John 1:12

This type of faith is described in Ephesians 2:8-9,

> *For by grace are ye saved through faith; and that not of yourselves: it is the gift of God:*
>
> *Not of works, lest any man should boast.*

In case you have never consciously confessed Jesus Christ by inviting Him into your heart as your personal Lord and Saviour, please turn to the end of this book right now to pray the salvation prayer and I assure you that you will become born again as soon as you say those words in faith.

Galatians 5 describes another kind of faith: **the fruit of faith or faithfulness.** This is a fruit of the Spirit, which grows in the life of a Christian to establish him in spiritual character and puts heaven into him. The Bible says,

> *But the fruit of the Spirit is love, joy, peace ... faith.*
>
> *Galatians 5:22*

This is the faith that believers have in God, in His Word and His promises which cause us to believe, trust and commit ourselves to Him, being fully assured and rejoicing in those promises. This distinguishing kind of faith is recorded in Hebrews 11, as it recalls the various exploits that men and women did by believing in God and His promises.

Sadly, this is the kind of faith that is lacking among many Christians today. It is the childlike faith to just simply trust the promises of God. It is recorded in Mark 16:14 that after Christ's resurrection,

> *...He appeared unto the eleven as they sat at meat, and upbraided them with their unbelief and hardness of heart, because they believed not them which had seen him after he was risen.*

They did not believe the witness of the women who said they saw the Lord, touched Him and held Him by the feet. In fact, Thomas said until he had seen and touched His nail-pierced hands, he would not believe (John 20:24-25). So, Jesus rebuked and upbraided them because of the hardness of their hearts to believe what

He promised He would do and what the women declared He had done. This explains why when Christ was walking with the two disciples on the road to Emmaus, He said to them, *O fools, and slow of heart to believe all that the prophets have spoken* (Luke 24:25).

This kind of faith can be increased and nurtured to grow. God's Word tells believers to *build themselves up on their most holy faith* (Jude 1:20). The scripture talks about increasing in faith. I believe that this kind of faith grows over time, as we experience more of the faithfulness of God in our own lives.

Really, it is one thing to read about what God did for those in the Bible; but oftentimes, we think of them as a special class and therefore believe we do not qualify like them. Do not forget that Elijah was a man of like passions, as we are; he prayed and it did not rain for the space of three years, then he prayed again, and it rained (James 5:17).

Certainly, as you see and experience the faithfulness of God to take care, provide for and guide you in different areas of life, this kind of faith and confidence in the promises of God and His Word keeps growing. As a result, you experience the reality of that faith. Your faith increases to the extent that life's situations do not disturb you anymore because you know it is all in God's hands and He will take care of it.

Another type of faith, which I will be discussing, is

the gift of faith. It is a gift of the Holy Spirit considered by many as the greatest of the three power gifts of the Spirit: the gift of faith, the working of miracles and the gift of healing. The gift of faith stems from saving faith and the fruit of faith, and it is the ability to believe God for the miraculous.

When the gift of faith is in operation, it enables one to have the supernatural capacity to believe God and His Word without doubt, deal with unbelief and envision what God wants to accomplish. It is also the supernatural ability to meet adverse circumstances with confidence in God's Word and messages by His prophets. With the gift of faith, you can display boldness in all situations. It is written,

> *But this I confess unto thee, that after the way which they call heresy, so worship I the God of my fathers, believing all things which are written in the law and in the prophets:*
>
> *Acts 24:14*

Doubtless, this manifestation of the gift of faith comes after the baptism of the Holy Spirit. In case you are not yet baptised in the Holy Spirit with the evidence of speaking in unknown tongues, please turn to the end of this book to learn the process. Pray the prayer there, believe God for the baptism, open your mouth and begin to give thanks to God from your heart. Then begin to speak in other tongues as the Holy Spirit gives you utterance.

Please note: Saving faith produces the active faith of the fruit of the Spirit, which in turn produces the gift of faith. When the gift of faith is empowered, the results are miraculous.

At this point, it is important to clearly state that the differences between the gifts of faith and the general faith that believers have is that general faith can be increased by feeding on the Word of God and exercising it in every area of your life. On the other hand, we don't all have the gift of faith; it is a supernatural manifestation.

Doubtless, the gift of faith empowers you for service and enables you to demonstrate God's power as a sign to the dying world.

The gift of faith is a special kind of faith given to the believer with which he or she passively receives a miracle. This is different from the working of miracles, where the believer actively works a miracle under the power of the Holy Spirit. Although, both gifts produce miracles, but the gift of faith is passive while the working of miracles is active.

At this point, let me show you some biblical examples of these gifts in action. When Elijah ascended to heaven, he dropped his mantle. Elisha, who had asked for a double portion of Elijah's anointing, saw that mantle, picked it up, and smote the waters, parting the Jordan hither and thither and he went over (2 Kings 2:14). He was actively operating the gift of faith in the working of miracles through the Spirit and power of God.

On the other hand, throughout Daniel's ministry, we see the passive gift of faith working many times. One example was when he received a miracle in the lions' den. In those days and all through history, people thrown into a lions' den were devoured (Daniel 6:16-24). Why didn't they devour Daniel? Well, the Bible says that Daniel believed God. God shut the mouths of the lions because of Daniel's faith and as a result, he wasn't hurt. That is the gift of faith in operation. Daniel didn't do anything. He probably just laid down and went to sleep among the lions knowing that there would be a special manifestation that would ensure his deliverance.

What was the end result for Daniel and Elisha? Both received a miracle, but they each received it in different ways. Elisha smote the river which was active; Daniel passively did nothing, but in faith and confidence, refused to give up whilst believing God for his rescue.

Those who operate this kind of faith can believe God in such a way that He honours their word as His own and miraculously brings to pass their desired result.

For instance, Elijah said, *By my word there shall be no rain* (1 Kings 17:1). True to his word, there was no rain on the earth for the space of three and a half years because God honoured his word. It was backed up with a special kind of faith that is beyond the realm of the usual and God confirmed this word as His (1 Kings 17:1, 7).

It was the gift of faith at work in Abraham that made him believe God that he would have a child, even when everything around him proved impossible. Though both he and his wife were past the age of childbearing, yet,

> *He staggered not at the promise of God through unbelief; but was strong in faith, giving glory to God;*
>
> Romans 4:20

In Matthew 8:23–27, Jesus exercised the gift of faith as He slept on a pillow in a ship during a raging storm. Jesus was not bothered by the storm just as Daniel was not bothered by the lions. They both laid down and slept right in the midst of danger. This is actually the common characteristic throughout the Bible of those who operated in this gift: the gift of faith primarily worked for individuals in the midst of danger and provided them with a calmness that was supernatural.

As I write this chapter, I remember this testimony of the only survivor of the Ethiopian Airline that crashed several years ago. In his testimony, he said that when the announcement of the crash landing was made by the pilot, he simply asked himself one question: 'What would my father in the faith, Bishop David Oyedepo, do in a situation like this?' He answered himself that he would maintain his calm. So, he took his mantle (anointed prayer cloth), which was blessed and prayed over by the Bishop sometime back, tied it around his neck and closed his eyes. After the plane crashed, he found himself inside the ocean floating, with an invisible hand holding him up, until he was washed ashore and eventually rescued. That's the gift of faith in operation.

Clearly, the gift of faith brings to pass the strange acts of God in our lives, thereby enabling us to command exploits. In Hebrews 11, there is a catalogue of people who exhibited this kind of faith.

Let me share this with you:

In 1982, God spoke to His servant, Dr. David O. Oyedepo that at the base of this ministry, a tent shall be built that will seat 50,000 (fifty thousand) people. Today, to the glory of God, at the international headquarters of this ministry, the 50,000-seat capacity Faith Tabernacle, which the Guinness Book of Records acknowledged as the largest Church Auditorium in the world, was built debt-free and within one year. This has become a reality among other things through the operation of the gift of faith.

As I write this today, four (4) services hold every Sunday in this world-renowned auditorium to the glory of God. Notably, this gift requires a bold declaration of your trust in God; it is not timid, neither does it waver. It declares whatever God has said in accordance with His Word, without any doubt. It believes that what the mouth of God has spoken, His hand will perform. There is a need for believers to possess this gift of faith for sweatless triumph in life.

Another operation of the gift of faith is supernatural sustenance in a time of famine, just as when Elijah was fed by the ravens (1 Kings 17:6). Elijah's faith had to be given to him supernaturally because it was beyond the Word of God to believe that ravens, who biologically do not feed their young, would feed him. Yet, that's exactly what happened: ravens brought him food, morning and night.

The gift of faith can also be employed in casting out evil spirits. You are trusting God to honour your word when you command a spirit to come out in the name of Jesus. You may notice, though, that other gifts of the Spirit are in operation in this situation as well. For instance, when someone casts out a demon, the gift of discerning of spirits and the gift of faith are in operation. Sometimes, the word of knowledge is at work as well. If you don't discern the spirit when you are casting out demons, very often it is revealed through the word of knowledge. Either way, the gift of faith still has to be exercised while casting out the spirit.

Beyond the saving faith, fruit of faith and the gift of faith, there is the spirit of faith. Wherever the **spirit of faith** is operational, nothing is impossible to the possessor. The spirit of faith makes you a co-creator with God because you can frame your world by this dimension of faith. It is written,

> ***Through faith we understand that the worlds were framed by the word of God, so that things which are seen were not made of things which do appear.***
> *Hebrews 11:3*

The kind of faith referred to in the above scripture is not just an ordinary faith, but the spirit of faith. It is a strong and potent force that delivers the impossible, unimaginable and strangest happenings to you. It brings you to the realm where you have whatsoever you say. For instance, Prophet Elijah in the Old Testament operated through the spirit of faith. That was why he could undoubtedly command fire to consume an altar that was impossible to be gutted by fire in its present circumstance (1 Kings 18:25-39).

Notably, the spirit of faith has two major qualities, without which it cannot be effective. It is a **believing** force, as well as a **speaking** force. Everyone who possesses the spirit of faith believes all things and speaks boldly what they believe. You are not afraid to declare a thing because you do not doubt its materialisation. Moreover, it is your bold declaration that performs what you believe in your heart. God is only committed to performing what you believe; however, it would only be done when you give voice to it.

The truth is: Whatever God's Word says, the spirit

of faith dares to believe and whatever the spirit of faith believes, it declares boldly. The Apostles said, *For we cannot but speak the things which we have seen and heard* (Acts 4:20), and we know that they commanded great signs and wonders through the operation of the spirit of faith in them.

Apostle Paul also operated by the spirit of faith and he said, *But this I confess unto thee, that after the way which they call heresy, so worship I the God of my fathers, believing all things which are written in the law and in the prophets* (Acts 24:14). His ability to believe all things was through the operation of the spirit of faith. The spirit of faith makes you believe God to do what He has promised, even when the situation seems unchanging.

The spirit of faith is a propeller of special miracles. Every strange and creative miracle you see today was compelled through the spirit of faith at work in a man. God uses men to perform His works on the earth, but He will only work through you by your faith. However, your level of faith determines your level of command of signs and wonders. Concerning Apostle Paul, the Bible says,

> *And God wrought special miracles by the hands of Paul:*
>
> *So that from his body were brought unto the sick handkerchiefs or aprons, and the diseases departed*

from them, and the evil spirits went out of them.
Acts 19:11-12

The spirit of faith enables you to command unquestionable victory in all endeavours and brings you to the realm of unlimited exploits. Faith is what moves God into action and the spirit of faith resides in your heart. Faith in God's Word, loaded in your heart and triggered by the words from your mouth, releases unprecedented breakthroughs. It is written,

We having the same spirit of faith, according as it is written, I believed, and therefore have I spoken; we also believe, and therefore speak;
2 Corinthians 4:13

Understand that the spirit of faith comes primarily from the Word of God and it is the Holy Spirit giving you insight to God's Word that stirs up faith in you. A deep knowledge of God's Word makes the spirit of faith effective in you.

The mere fact that you are born again does not guarantee you victory over the devil and all his evil devices. However, by the spirit of faith, you can overcome every opposition from the pit of hell (1 John 5:14).

Please note that there is more to the subject on the spirit of faith than what is written in this book. However, you can learn more from my book titled, **The Spirit of Faith**.

God's General, Smith Wigglesworth, said that oftentimes, if you will take a step of faith and use the general faith you have as a Christian, when you come to the end of that faith, very often, supernatural faith will take over or kick in. The reason it hasn't happened like this for a lot of believers today is because they don't first use what they already have.

The Gifts of Healing

> *...To another the gifts of healing by the same Spirit.*
> *1 Corinthians 12:9*

In the above scripture, the Bible talks about the 'gifts' of healing because there are different types of healings: physical healing (from sicknesses and diseases such as blindness, deafness, cancer, diabetes, HIV/AIDS, etc.), emotional healing (such as from overt anxiety, jealousy, discouragement, bitterness, greed, guilt and other destructive attitudes) and spiritual healing (such as from gross prayerlessness, lack of Word study, etc.).

The gifts of healing is an extraordinary and supernatural enabling given to a believer to minister various kinds of healing and restoration of health to individuals, through the power of the Holy Spirit. With this gift at work in you, you cheaply exercise dominion over all sicknesses and diseases.

This spiritual gift is closely related to the gifts of faith and working of miracles. Although all spiritual gifts are to be exercised in faith, the gifts of healing involve a special measure of it. It is a gift you are endowed with that engraces you to heal other people. This gift is quite interesting because there is no guarantee that a person will always be able to heal anyone he or she desires. It is subject to the sovereign will of God, as all spiritual gifts are God's ultimate desire, just as it was evident during the earthly ministry of Jesus that He healed all. The Bible says,

> *How God anointed Jesus of Nazareth with the Holy Ghost and with power: who went about doing good, and healing all that were oppressed of the devil; for God was with him.*
>
> *Acts 10:38*

The spiritual gifts of healing reveal the heart and compassion of God. There were Old Testament manifestations of God's healing as well as the promises and the declaration by God that He is the Lord who heals His people (Exodus 15:26). Through healings, among other things, God revealed that He was near to His people and He cared about their sufferings. In the New Testament, one of the prominent features of the ministry of Jesus Christ was the healing of the sick. He healed countless number of people and cast out the demons tormenting them with sicknesses and diseases (Matthew 4:23-24, 8:16, 9:35; Mark 1:34).

This gift puts you in command over all forms of sicknesses and diseases. Jesus who was in full operation of this gift was doubtlessly in command of sickness; He went about healing all that were oppressed of the devil by this gift at work in Him (Acts 10:38), He gave the disciples power in Mark 6:7,

And he called unto him the twelve, and began to send them forth by two and two; and gave them power over unclean spirits.

And in Mark 6:12-13,

And they went out, and preached that men should repent.

And they cast out many devils, and anointed with oil many that were sick, and healed them.

This gift was also very prominent in the New Testament church and God was working in the church confirming their words with signs following. A prominent aspect of their ministry, when they went out to preach the gospel, was the healing of the sick.

In Acts 3, there is the amazing healing of a man seen and known by all as being lame from his mother's womb. That man's healing gave the disciples an opportunity to preach about Jesus and His crucifixion to the people.

It is written,

And a certain man lame from his mother's womb

was carried, whom they laid daily at the gate of the temple which is called Beautiful, to ask alms of them that entered into the temple;

Who seeing Peter and John about to go into the temple asked an alms.

Then Peter said, ... In the name of Jesus Christ of Nazareth rise up and walk.

And he took him by the right hand, and lifted him up: and immediately his feet and ankle bones received strength.

And he leaping up stood, and walked, ...

And as the lame man which was healed held Peter and John, all the people ran together unto them in the porch that is called Solomon's, greatly wondering.

And when Peter saw it, he answered unto the people, ... Repent ye therefore, and be converted, that your sins may be blotted out, when the times of refreshing shall come from the presence of the Lord;

This gift was so much at work in Peter that even his shadow healed the sick! The Bible records,

Insomuch that they brought forth the sick into the streets, and laid them on beds and couches, that at the least the shadow of Peter passing by might overshadow some of them.

Acts 5:15

Paul also walked in the full manifestation of this gift such that,

> *...God wrought special miracles by the hands of Paul:*
>
> *So that from his body were brought unto the sick handkerchiefs or aprons, and the diseases departed from them, and the evil spirits went out of them.*
>
> Acts 19:11-12

Without any doubt, gifts of healing work in the church of God today. A brother testified at the Faith Tabernacle, sometime ago:

On Thursday, at 8:00 a.m., I discovered that my son could neither turn his neck nor walk. I rejected the situation and took him to the hospital. The doctor treated him for malaria and when we got home, he was able to move his neck.

The following Thursday, he stopped walking. I returned to the hospital for treatment, yet afterwards, he still could not walk. A doctor referred me to Bishop David Oyedepo after confiding in another doctor that my son was paralysed. I immediately rejected his doctoral report and ran to the church.

When I saw the Bishop, I ran to him. I couldn't even say anything, because I was shivering and weeping. When the Bishop asked me what the matter was, I said, 'Your son, your son!' I gave him the doctor's report, but he didn't read it; rather, he squeezed it and said, 'No! It can't be!'

Immediately, he said, 'Bring your child!' He held my son's legs, prayed and breathed on his legs. On Saturday of that same week, I woke up in the morning and saw my son running! — **Ajibola, P.**

The manifestations of the gifts of healing is different from what could be termed 'healing faith'. In Luke 8:42-48, we see the story of Jesus on His way to the house of Jairus whose daughter had died. As the crowd who followed Him kept pushing Him, suddenly, Jesus stopped and asked, 'Who touched Me?' Peter's response in verse 45 was, **Master, the multitude throng thee and press thee, and sayest thou, Who touched me?** But Jesus said, **Somebody hath touched me: for I perceive that virtue is gone out of me.**

Then, the woman with the issue of blood came and knelt before Him trembling and confessed how she touched the hem of His garment and immediately was healed. Jesus said, **'Daughter, be of good comfort: [your] faith hath made [you] whole…'**. That is classified as healing faith; that is, faith to be healed.

In Matthew 15:28, there was a woman from the area of Tyre who came to Jesus concerning her daughter, who she said was grievously vexed by the devil. When the disciples said, 'Lord do something. She is troubling us',

He replied them saying, 'I am not sent but to the lost sheep of the house of Israel'. Then the woman came directly to Jesus saying 'Lord, help me'. Scripture says,

> **But he answered and said, It is not meet to take the children's bread, and to cast it to dogs.**
>
> **And she said, Truth, Lord: yet the dogs eat of the crumbs which fall from their masters' table.**
>
> **Then Jesus answered and said unto her, O woman, great is thy faith: be it unto thee even as thou wilt. And her daughter was made whole from that very hour.**
>
> *Matthew 15:26-28*

That healing faith is the woman's faith that brought healing to her little daughter.

Another example of healing faith is in Mark 10:46-52; it tells of Blind Bartimaeus, the son of Timaeus, who sat by the highway side begging. When he heard that Jesus of Nazareth was passing by, he began to cry out, 'Jesus, thou Son of David, have mercy on me'. In response to his ceaseless, unstoppable cry, Jesus stood still, and commanded him to be called. Jesus said unto him, 'What wilt thou that I should do unto thee'? The blind man said unto Him, 'Lord, that I might receive my sight'. And Jesus said unto him, 'Go thy way; thy faith hath made thee whole'. Immediately, he received his sight and followed Jesus in the way.

Clearly, there is a very close relationship between

the healing faith and the gifts of healing. The main difference however is: Whilst the healing faith requires the faith of the recipient for healing, the gifts of healing involves God supernaturally endowing the person He wants to use as a channel, with the dimension of faith that believes in the invincible power of God to work special miracles.

It is important to note at this point that without you having great compassion, you cannot operate in the gifts of healing. The gift is not an act of showmanship or a proof of your level of spirituality or command; rather, it is God working through you to break the hold of satan operating with the spirit of infirmity in the lives of people. You must covet this gift with passion and a crave to see people saved, delivered and liberated from the activities of satan and his cohorts.

The Gift of Working of Miracles

To another the working of miracles.

1 Corinthians 12:10

We have examined the gift of faith and the gifts of healing and how these two gifts go together. Also tied to the gift of faith is the gift of working of miracles. The ultimate purpose of these power gifts of faith, healing and the working of miracles is to exercise authority over satan, sickness, sin and the binding forces of this age.

A miracle can be defined as either a creative work or a

supernatural act of the Holy Spirit that defies the laws of nature and cannot be explained by logic. It is the supernatural power to do things which are otherwise humanly impossible but divinely simple. It is doing a supernatural act that man cannot naturally do. It is the performance of something which is against the law of nature. It is the supernatural power to intervene and counteract earthly and evil forces.

The gift of 'working of miracles' means the energising power to work a miracle. There is a 'work or working' involved in this gift and not simply receiving miracles. It is a supernatural manifestation of the power of God that alters or changes, suspends or lays aside, or in some other way controls the laws of nature; it is a supernatural ability given by the Holy Spirit. It is the operation of the power of God upon material things; it operates upon man's environment, as a sign and wonder. Notably, God usually manifests this gift in blessing, but sometimes also in judgment. For example, most of the plagues of Egypt occurred through the gift of working of miracles.

Please understand: The gift of working of miracles occurs as the Holy Spirit wills – at the right time, when and where He wills. It is the empowering of the believer by the Holy Spirit to meet a need at a particular time; an operation of God's power that changes natural law and material things, and produces seen miraculous effects.

This gift represents the mighty power of God flowing in the life of a person, thereby causing great miracles to occur. By the gift of working of miracles, the Holy Spirit manifests the power of God through the believer, which makes the seemingly impossible happen. Read this scripture carefully,

> **And God wrought special miracles by the hands of Paul.**
>
> *Acts 19:11*

It is this ability to perform special miracles that is called the gift of working of miracles. It acknowledges the extraordinary hand of God in the life of a man. For instance, how would you explain a person born with Sickle Cell Anaemia (SS), a condition that is medically incurable, but through the special miracle of God, has their genotype turned to AA?

It is not in the realm of knowledge, edifying gifts, physical healing or the gift of faith. The gift of working of miracles is God empowering the believer to act in the name of Jesus.

Somehow, the working of miracles is said to be the least common of the gifts of power. It demands a very close walk with God as sin and failure can greatly hinder God's plans and desires.

The realm of the miraculous is the realm of the supernatural where everything is made possible by the power of God, because it enables you to live above impossibilities. The Bible is full of miracles and probably the biggest of these start in the very first verse, Genesis 1:1, *In the beginning God created the heavens and the earth.* Think of this: God, who is big enough to create the whole universe, is big enough to do anything! Difficulty has to be measured by the capacity of the agent that is doing the work. When God is the Agent doing the work, the possibility of difficulty is absurd.

The working of miracles can be a provision in the time of need, such as a car continuing to run without petrol as Pastor E. A. Adeboye (the General Overseer of the Redeemed Christian Church of God) testifies of or food that multiplies as was the case with the widow of Zarephath, whose last oil and flour never finished all through the famine (1 Kings 17:10-15). When there is no means of natural provision, the Lord is able to provide through the working of miracles.

The working of miracles can be a creative work of the Holy Spirit. A withered hand once grew out at one of our church services at the Faith Tabernacle in Canaanland. This creative testimony below will also inspire you as you read it.

I had my son seven months ago, but he was diagnosed with hydro cell (collection of fluid in the scrotum).

When Bishop David Oyedepo prayed during one of the Shiloh services on December 12, 2014, my son who didn't have testes developed two new ones.

In addition, throughout this time, I stopped going to work so I could participate in soul winning outreaches. When I went, I took my baby along. However, for the last seven months that I was out of work, I received my full salary.

Also, all my siblings are now members of Winners' Chapel including my husband. I give thanks to God!
— **Judith, A.**

The working of miracles can be a restoration of life or resurrection from the dead. Paul the Apostle said to King Agrippa, **Why should it be thought a thing incredible with you, that God should raise the dead?** (Acts 26:8). It is not a problem for God to raise the dead, because He breathed life into Adam when he was just an inanimate matter made out of mud in the first place!

It is reported that at least fourteen (14) people were raised from the dead under the ministry of Smith Wigglesworth. It was a common phenomenon in the ministry of Archbishop Benson Idahosa. In this ministry today, many of such encounters have been recorded. There is the particular example of Brother Obara:

In June 1999, my wife convinced me to join Winners' Chapel, at the Faith Tabernacle, Canaanland. Since we joined, we experienced victorious testimonies.

However, on March 2, I travelled to Abuja. Before I left, I prayed with my family. On getting to Lokoja, I ran out of fuel. So, I parked at a fuel station to pass the night so I could look for fuel the following day.

During the night, a trailer carrying a container drove towards my vehicle. The container fell off the trailer and crushed my car, trapping me in it for hours. When the rescue team arrived, I was certified dead.

The container also hit another stationary vehicle, containing 18 passengers and everyone in that bus died. So, we were all taken to Lokoja General Hospital.

Before then, I attended the February Breakthrough Summit, with the theme: Commanding Supernatural Victory. I bought the audio tapes of the summit and was listening to one of them before I slept. In my dream, I kept hearing a statement that Bishop Oyedepo made in that tape: 'There is no champion without stories of challenges to tell. So, wake up!'

Meanwhile, a pastor from Kaduna drove past and saw my crushed vehicle with the Winners' sticker. He came to the hospital and asked the hospital management to allow him see the accident victims. They took him to the mortuary and miraculously, on bringing me out, they discovered that I was alive!

Also, the Breakthrough Summit tape was wrapped round my arm like a bandage, and that was the only part of my body that had no scar from the accident. Against the doctor's recommendation that I stay in the hospital for three months, supernatural strength came into me and I left the hospital for Lagos that day. I give glory to God! —**Obara, M. O.**

What a mighty God we serve! The gift of working of miracles can provide divine protection. A supernatural deliverance can take place when all natural possibilities of deliverance are gone. For instance, there was an experience my husband once had, driving on a narrow bride late one night, while driving to Northern Nigeria for a meeting years ago. Already on the bridge, too small to take two vehicles at the same time, he noticed an oncoming trailer; with no option to reverse and make it out of the bridge in time, there was sudden unexplainable rescue! That was indeed a miracle!

Sadly, there are Christians who do not believe such things can happen today, but why should it be thought strange for God to work miracles today when they are seen all through scripture?

In the Old Testament, there were many miracles in the life of Moses and the gift of the working of miracles surely was something that Moses possessed. With the Egyptians, there was the turning of the river to blood, the flies, the boils upon the Egyptians and then the frogs. There was the miracle of God showing His approval upon

Aaron as the high priest and his family (Numbers 17). Through the prayers of Elijah, a child was restored to life. There was the multiplying of the oil with the woman who was poor (1 Kings 17). Another miracle occurred when the spring in Jericho was healed (2 Kings 2).

Moving to the New Testament and the life of Jesus, we have so many miracles recorded. They began at the feast of Cana in Galilee when Jesus turned water to wine (John 2). He healed the nobleman's son from a distance (Matthew 8:13), He raised the dead son of the widow of Nain (Luke 7:13-15), He raised the dead daughter of Jairus (Mark 5:41-42). Then, He raised Lazarus, who had been buried for four days, from the dead (John 11:43-44) and He fed multitudes with five loaves and two fishes (Luke 9:16-17). Then, He walked on water (Matthew 14:25). These are marvellous miracles.

When Paul was writing to the Corinthians defending the title of apostle, he said to them in 2 Corinthians 12:12, *Truly the signs of an apostle were wrought among you in all patience, in signs and wonders and mighty deeds.* So, Paul was pointing to the miracles that were performed through his ministry while he was in Corinth. And he used those to attest to the fact that he was an Apostle. Thus, it seems that it was one of the evidences of apostleship in the early church to have the gift of working of miracles.

The Apostles regularly performed miracles of all kinds

including casting out demons, healings, raising people from the dead and much more (Acts 2:43, 3:1-10, 5:1-16, 9:36-43, 13:4-12, 19:11-12). Stephen, full of faith and power, did great wonders and miracles among the people (Acts 6:8). Philip, one of those chosen to wait on the tables, went to Samaria to preach Christ and many believed, and were baptised when they saw the miracles that he did (Acts 8:5-6). But the gift of the working of miracles is not limited to the Apostles. For instance, Ananias, a disciple not an apostle, was used of God to restore Saul's sight in Acts 9.

Doubtless, God is a miracle working God! The time of the gifts of the Holy Spirit has not passed, and these signs still follow those who believe; you can be one of such!

Our ministry has been privileged of God to be a partaker of this from inception. I can boldly testify that all manner of miracles have, and still take place regularly, in increasing dimension; the dead have been raised and even hands or legs that were physically unequal, have grown to became equal.

As God's General, Dr T. L. Osborn rightly said: 'Speaking in tongues is not enough. If we turn men from unchristian religions to Christianity, we must produce miracles which convince men that Christ lives and He is real today'.

Therefore, just like me, you must continuously deeply

desire to show proofs of your spirituality by engaging effectively the power of the Holy Spirit in you.

Remember: Miracles bring glory to God, bring the lost to the saving knowledge of Jesus Christ and demonstrate with visible outward signs the truth of God's Word. It is to convince unbelievers that God's Word is true, and that Jesus is truly the way of salvation and the only way to God!

The Holy Spirit: His Gifts III

In this chapter, by the help of the Holy Spirit, we shall be examining the vocal gifts.

THE VOCAL GIFTS

To another the working of miracles; to another prophecy; to another discerning of spirits; to another divers kinds of tongues; to another the interpretation of tongues.

1 Corinthians 12:10

These gifts are speaking gifts and they are also referred to as the gifts of inspiration or utterance. They have nothing to do with your communication skill or intellectual capacity; it is a vocal miracle of the Holy Spirit. They are designed to edify, build-up and strengthen the church, not just the individual, and their distribution within the body is dependent upon the Holy Spirit, not man. It is written,

Even so ye, forasmuch as ye are zealous of spiritual gifts,
seek that ye may excel to the edifying of the church.

1 Corinthians 14:12

Unlike the revelation and power gifts, the vocal gifts are essentially for the benefit of others, even though those who have these gifts also benefit from them. We all need edification and strengthening and that is what happens when we prophesy, speak in diverse kinds of tongues and interpret those tongues as the Holy Spirit gives utterance.

Let's briefly examine each of these vocal gifts.

The Gift of Prophecy

For the prophecy came not in old time by the will
of man: but holy men of God spake as they were
moved by the Holy Ghost.

2 Peter 1:21

Prophecy is an inspired utterance from the Holy Spirit, through a gifted vessel. It is distinct from the gift of wisdom or knowledge because it is a direct message from God that is not always conscious to the one with the gift. Yet, the one with the gift feels compelled to share the truth revealed by God with others. It is a special ability that God gives to certain members of the body of Christ to receive and communicate an immediate message from God to His gathered people, a group among them, or any one of His people individually through a divinely anointed utterance, with such authority and urgency that can be perceived by the hearers.

The Bible records a fascinating instance in Luke 1:67-69,

> *And his father Zacharias was filled with the Holy Ghost, and prophesied, saying,*
>
> *Blessed be the Lord God of Israel; for he hath visited and redeemed his people,*
>
> *And hath raised up an horn of salvation for us in the house of his servant David.*

This gift is a communication gift and those with the gift of prophecy will often feel as though they have a direct word from God that will comfort, encourage, guide, warn or rebuke the body of Christ or an individual.

Really, it is a supernatural speech in a known language. It is usually said in an instance and is not premeditated. It is an inspiration, a flash, with words chosen by the Holy Spirit and not by the individual.

Prophecy speaks to the understanding of those involved and it is a message from God to men. The word of prophecy is usually brought to a group of believers or an individual, and can be proved by the church. This is why it is important to be able to discern spirits, so you can effectively weigh if the prophecy received is from God.

To prophesy is to speak under divine inspiration; not

merely to predict future events, but to deliver as the instrument of the Holy Ghost, the messages of God to men, whether in the form of doctrine, exhortation or consolation. It is written,

> *But he that prophesieth speaketh unto men to edification, and exhortation, and comfort.*
>
> *1 Corinthians 14:3*

The gift of prophecy as found in the above scripture is firstly for **edification,** which means to strengthen or build-up. Prophecy touches the church at its point of need. In a scriptural sense, it is a revelation of God's love, care and desire for His people to be built-up in their walk and relationship with Christ. It is not to be used to criticise or condemn.

Secondly, the gift of prophecy is for **exhortation**; that is, to charge into action. There are a lot of things that we believe, but we are passive in our reaction to them. For instance, we know that we should pray but we do not always pray. We know that we should be worshipping the Lord but we do not always worship Him. We know that we should be faithful but we are not always faithful. So, by the gift of prophecy we are exhorted to pray, praise, trust the Lord or love as the scripture commands.

The Bible clearly exhorts all believers in James 1:22-25,

> *But be ye doers of the word, and not hearers only,*

deceiving your own selves.

For if any be a hearer of the word, and not a doer, he is like unto a man beholding his natural face in a glass:

For he beholdeth himself, and goeth his way, and straightway forgetteth what manner of man he was.

But whoso looketh into the perfect law of liberty, and continueth therein, he being not a forgetful hearer, but a doer of the work, this man shall be blessed in his deed.

That clearly is an exhortation which spurs you to take action that brings you into dimensions of blessings in response to your deeds.

Thirdly, the gift is for **comfort**, which means a consolation or solace ministered with tenderness. 'Consolation' is 'to alleviate grief or disappointment' and 'solace' is 'to comfort in distress or disappointment, find relief and cheer up'. There is comfort in knowing that God is in control, He is on the throne and He rules. A person experiencing tests, trials, tribulations and hardships will find it quite comforting to know that God is on the throne because in times of challenges, it is very easy to forget that God loves us enough to care about our situations.

It is, therefore, comforting to be reminded that the Lord understands and knows our circumstances, especially when we are sometimes tempted to think that things are out of hand. With this gift at work, it becomes easy to understand that God is watching over you and He will bring you through victoriously.

Paul the Apostle speaks of the comfort that God gives, calling God, 'the God of all comforts', who comforts us with the comfort wherewith we are able to comfort others. It is written,

> **Blessed be God, even the Father of our Lord Jesus Christ, the Father of mercies, and the God of all comfort;**
>
> **Who comforteth us in all our tribulation, that we may be able to comfort them which are in any trouble, by the comfort wherewith we ourselves are comforted of God.**
>
> *2 Corinthians 1:3-4*

Conclusively, the gift of prophecy is primarily for the profiting of the church or an individual, to bring us to the perfect will of God.

The Hebrew meaning of the word, 'to prophesy' is 'to flow forth'. The Greek word that is translated as 'prophecy' means 'to speak for another'. So, prophecy can mean a word spoken on God's behalf to His people as prompted by Him.

However, it is important to state clearly here that having the gift of prophecy does not make you a prophet because the office of the prophet is different from the gift of prophecy. All may prophesy but all cannot be prophets. For instance, Philip's four daughters in Acts 21:9 manifested this gift, but they were not prophets. Thus, just like Paul admonished, we should desire the gift of prophecy whereby we would understand and speak the mind of Christ at all times. It is written,

> *I would that ye all spake with tongues, but rather that ye prophesied: for greater is he that prophesieth than he that speaketh with tongues, except he interpret, that the church may receive edifying.*
>
> *1 Corinthians 14:5*

The Gift of Diverse Kinds of Tongues

> *...To another divers kinds of tongues...*
> *1 Corinthians 12:10*

The gift of diverse kinds of tongues is an utterance spoken audibly by the Spirit, in the midst of others, in a language that is not learnt or understood by the speaker. It is the Holy Spirit giving you the supernatural ability to speak in an unknown tongue that you have no knowledge or ability to speak on your own naturally. The Bible says that he that speaks in an unknown tongue speaks mysteries. Read this scripture carefully,

> *For he that speaketh in an unknown tongue speaketh not unto men, but unto God: for no man understandeth him; howbeit in the spirit he speaketh mysteries.*
>
> *1 Corinthians 14:2*

There is a clear difference between the gift of diverse kinds of tongues and speaking in tongues as evidence of Holy Ghost baptism. The gift of tongues is for public assembly and should always be accompanied by the gift of interpretation of tongues. The rare exception to this is when God speaks to an individual through the person speaking. In other words, one person will speak with the gift of tongues but to the person, to whom the message is addressed, it will be in a language he or she understands.

Speaking with tongues, on the other hand, is for your personal spiritual enrichment. You receive personal edification and supernatural build-ups by speaking in other tongues. It does not need an interpretation like the gift of tongues does, because it is simply you speaking to God.

According to 1 Corinthians 13:1, there are two types of tongues – the tongues of men and of angels,

> *Though I speak with the tongues of men and of angels, and have not charity, I am become as sounding brass, or a tinkling cymbal.*

The first type is the tongues of men, which is a tongue of this earth. For instance, if your native language is English, then the Holy Spirit can give you the ability to speak in Chinese, Japanese, or Spanish. This was what happened on the day of Pentecost when the believers were baptised with the Holy Ghost and began to speak in tongues and prophesy (Acts 2). This was a sign to the unbelievers who did not know Christ, as they were shocked to hear these Galileans speak to every Jew present in his own native language, though they had never learned it.

Read this scripture carefully,

> *And they were all amazed and marvelled, saying one to another, Behold, are not all these which speak Galilaeans?*
>
> *And how hear we every man in our own tongue, wherein we were born?*
>
> *Parthians, and Medes, and Elamites, and the dwellers in Mesopotamia, and in Judaea, and Cappadocia, in Pontus, and Asia,*
>
> *Phrygia, and Pamphylia, in Egypt, and in the parts of Libya about Cyrene, and strangers of Rome, Jews and proselytes,*
>
> *Cretes and Arabians, we do hear them speak in our tongues the wonderful works of God.*
>
> *Acts 2:7-11*

The second type of tongue is a tongue directly from heaven, a heavenly language that is not of this earth. 1 Corinthians 13 refers to it as the **tongues of angels.** The scripture states,

> *Likewise the Spirit also helpeth our infirmities: for we know not what we should pray for as we ought: but the Spirit itself maketh intercession for us with*

groanings which cannot be uttered.

Romans 8:26

In other words, our language and knowledge are limited. However, when we yield ourselves to the Holy Spirit, He utilises our lips, tongues and voices to pray in the heavenly prayer language. He knows what to pray for according to the will of God (Romans 8:27). So, we pray voluntarily, but the Holy Spirit gives us the language by which we do so (groanings which we cannot utter – something that is not our native tongue; not learned).

Likewise, the Holy Spirit helps our infirmities; weaknesses and limitations (Romans 8:26). Remember: When you speak in an unknown tongue, you edify and build up yourself (1 Corinthians 14:4; Jude 1:20). You can recharge your spirit, much like a battery gets charged. Have you ever felt like you are having a bad day or lack wisdom for a particular situation? At such times, pray in tongues and the Holy Ghost will help your weaknesses and limitations; He will empower you. 1 Corinthians 14:22 states,

Wherefore tongues are for a sign, not to them that believe, but to them that believe not: but prophesying serveth not for them that believe not, but for them which believe.

Please understand: The infilling of the Holy Spirit with

the evidence of speaking in tongues is the foundation of this gift. So, to manifest this gift, you have to first be baptised with the Holy Ghost.

Worthy of note is that after Jesus breathed on His disciples and told them, *Receive ye the Holy Ghost* in John 20:22, He commanded these same disciples in Acts 1:4-5, *...That they should not depart from Jerusalem, but wait for the promise of the Father, which, saith he, ye have heard of me. For John truly baptized with water; but ye shall be baptized with the Holy Ghost not many days hence.*

He did not want them to depart from Jerusalem as witnesses for Him until they received the power from on high (Holy Spirit baptism), which is still His charge to every one of us today. Why? This is because Holy Ghost baptism would enable you to be led by the Spirit of God in all you do (especially when witnessing to people), and operate in the nine gifts of the Spirit spoken of in 1 Corinthians 12:8-10. It will empower your prayer life by adding excitement to prayers, fortify your energy on the prayer altar and enable you to be taught and guided by the Holy Spirit. It will further enable you to sing and give thanks effectively in the Spirit using the heavenly prayer language which Paul the Apostle referred to as the 'language of angels' (1 Corinthians 14:15, 17). Isn't that wonderful?

Please understand: An easy way to remember the

difference between speaking with tongues, as evidence of Holy Ghost baptism, and the gift of tongues, is that speaking with tongues is man talking to God; it goes from earth to heaven. The gift of tongues, on the other hand, comes from heaven to earth, because it is God speaking through a man to other men.

The Gift of Interpretation of Tongues

If any man speak in an [unknown] tongue, let it be by two, or at the most by] three, and that by course; and let one interpret.

But if there be no interpreter, let him keep silence in the church; and let him speak to himself, and to God.

1 Corinthians 14:27-28

Clearly, the gift of diverse tongues will be irrelevant if it is not interpreted. Every gift of diverse tongues manifested in church must of necessity be interpreted, bearing in mind that the purpose of the gifts of the Holy Spirit is for the edification and profiting of the church.

This interpretation is not a word-for-word translation of the tongue, but it gives the meaning of the tongue in a language that can be understood. The Bible says,

Wherefore let him that speaketh in an unknown tongue pray that he may interpret.

1 Corinthians 14:13

Without the gift of interpretation of tongues, the gifts

of speaking in diverse tongues will be unfruitful. As I have stated earlier, every gift of the Holy Spirit is to edify, but we cannot be edified if we do not understand the message given. As it is written,

> *For if the trumpet give an uncertain sound, who shall prepare himself to the battle?*
>
> *So likewise ye, except ye utter by the tongue words easy to be understood, how shall it be known what is spoken? For ye shall speak into the air.*
>
> *1 Corinthians 14:8-9*

Doubtless, the purpose of the gift of interpretation of tongues is to give meaning to the gift of diverse tongues, so that the hearer can understand and be edified. One way to judge if this interpretation is of the Holy Spirit is that it would strengthen, inspire and bless the hearer and not bring confusion to them, because God is not the author of confusion (1 Corinthians 14:33).

It is also important to know that sometimes, it is possible to interpret your own tongues as you pray. The Holy Spirit may sometimes cause you to speak in diverse tongues while you pray and also give you the interpretation as a direct message to you. It is written,

> *Wherefore let him that speaketh in an unknown tongue pray that he may interpret.*
>
> *For if I pray in an unknown tongue, my spirit prayeth, but my understanding is unfruitful.*
>
> *1 Corinthians 14:13-14*

But, Why the Gifts of the Holy Spirit?

To manifest the body of Christ on earth

Think of this: Just as the human body has many members with various functions, so is the body of Christ. There are different ministries, having various functions, but all to attain a defined purpose; that is, to perfect the will of God on the earth. The Bible clearly states,

> *For as we have many members in one body, and all members have not the same office:*
>
> *So we, being many, are one body in Christ, and every one members one of another.*
>
> *Having then gifts differing according to the grace that is given to us, whether prophecy, let us prophesy according to the proportion of faith;*
>
> *Or ministry, let us wait on our ministering: or he that teacheth, on teaching;*
>
> *Or he that exhorteth, on exhortation: he that giveth, let him do it with simplicity; he that ruleth, with diligence; he that sheweth mercy, with cheerfulness.*
>
> Romans 12:4-8

The gifts of the Spirit are to help the church manifest in these various arms of ministry. Ministry here does not refer to preaching or pastoral calling; it refers to your assignment on the earth and the purpose for which God created you. Everyone has a purpose and the manifestation of these gifts is to bring that purpose to its full realisation. The Bible says,

> **For the earnest expectation of the creature waiteth for the manifestation of the sons of God.**
>
> *Romans 8:19*

Please understand: The church of God is ordained to rule on the earth, but not without power. These gifts represent God's power to believers, which will enable them rule and dominate all the forces of darkness. With the manifestation of these gifts in you, every opposition against your rising is levelled out and you occupy your God-ordained place in destiny.

For effective evangelism

The gifts of the Holy Spirit also help to boost the work of evangelism. They serve as a sign to them who believe not. With the manifestation of these gifts, they would practically see the power of God at work, which would make them believe. The Bible says,

> **Then said Jesus unto him, Except ye see signs and wonders, ye will not believe.**
>
> *John 4:48*

So, the gifts of the Spirit are to bring the unbelievers to acknowledge the manifestation of the truth and as such, draw them closer to God.

For the edification of the church

The gifts also strengthen, build and uphold the church of God against the wiles of the enemy, help discern the right and acceptable will of God, and create a stronger fellowship between God and His church. As it is written,

> *Even so ye, forasmuch as ye are zealous of spiritual gifts, seek that ye may excel to the edifying of the church.*
>
> 1 Corinthians 14:12

It is important to understand that the gift is not for personal gain, but is beneficial to the carrier of it. It is also to unify the church of God, by giving everyone the power to function and grow in their various capacities.

For deliverance, protection and perfecting the church

Just like through the gift of the word of knowledge, Peter could tell by the Holy Spirit that Ananias and his wife lied, thereby exposing and preventing such act from creeping into the church, so it is with other gifts. They are for the profiting of the saints, by protecting the church from the devices of the enemy. Scripture says,

> *Put on the whole armour of God, that ye may be able to stand against the wiles of the devil.*
>
> Ephesians 6:11

As I conclude this chapter, let us briefly examine the difference between the fruit and the gift of the Holy

Spirit.

Spiritual fruit is <u>produced from within</u> while spiritual gifts are <u>imparted from without</u>. The gifts of the Holy Spirit are ministering gifts imparted to make believers function appropriately in the various ministry offices of the Church, that is, Christian service, while the fruit relates to the Christ-like character a believer should possess.

The **fruit** of the Spirit is **personal**. It is what every believer is supposed to be made up of, as it showcases you as a child of God. For instance, the Bible enjoins us to follow peace with all men and believers are also to portray the character of God which is love (Hebrews 12:14; 1 John 3:23; 2 Corinthians 13:11). This is what makes salvation genuine. But the **gift** of the Spirit is **not personal**; it is for the benefit of the whole body of Christ (1 Corinthians 12:1-31).

1 Corinthians 13 makes it clear that spiritual gifts without spiritual fruits are worthless. Fruit is eternal, but gifts are temporal (1 Corinthians 13:8); the former is a true measure of spirituality, but the latter is not.

Spiritual gifts are not the same as natural talents. Unlike the natural abilities which everyone has from birth, spiritual gifts belong exclusively to believers in Christ. In some cases, the gifts of the Spirit coincide with natural endowments, but they transcend natural abilities by adding a supernatural quality. Both are given by God; therefore, they should be developed and used according to their purpose for the glory of God (James 1:17; 1 Corinthians 10:31).

May your life benefit the body of Christ so that in everything, God will be glorified through Jesus Christ (1 Peter 4:11)!

Accessing The Power Of The Holy Spirit

O God, thou art my God; early will I seek thee: my soul thirsteth for thee, my flesh longeth for thee in a dry and thirsty land, where no water is;

To see thy power and thy glory, so as I have seen thee in the sanctuary.

Psalm 63:1-2

The power of the Holy Spirit is real and primarily for your benefit. However, for you to access it, certain things must be in place. Let us briefly examine some of them in this chapter.

Be Born Again

This means to confess your sins and accept Jesus Christ as your Lord and personal Saviour. It is only those who are truly born again that have access to the Holy Spirit, because He is the believer's seal (Ephesians 1:13). On the day of Pentecost, Peter and the Apostles were asked '**...Men and brethren what shall we do?**' Peter said, '**...Repent ...and ye shall receive the gift of the Holy Ghost**' (Acts 2:37-38).

And,

> *But the natural man receiveth not the things of the Spirit of God: for they are foolishness unto him: neither can he know them, because they are spiritually discerned.*
>
> *1 Corinthians 2:14*

If you are not born again, you cannot receive the Holy Spirit and without the Spirit, you are powerless. My question to you at this point is: Are you genuinely born again? Think deeply on this scripture,

> *Behold, I stand at the door, and knock: if any man hear my voice, and open the door, I will come in to him, and will sup with him, and he with me.*
>
> *Revelation 3:20*

In case you are not yet born again, which means you have not consciously received Jesus into your heart as your personal Lord and Saviour, please say the salvation prayer at the end of this book before you continue reading.

Thirst For It

> *O God, thou art my God; early will I seek thee: my soul thirsteth for thee, my flesh longeth for thee in*

a dry and thirsty land, where no water is.

Psalm 63:1

Only those who genuinely thirst for the baptism of the Holy Spirit qualify to be filled. To thirst means to desire a thing with desperation. Jesus talking about the Holy Spirit said, if any man thirst let him come and with this thirst comes a filling (John 7:37-39).

The truth is: What you do not truly desire holds no value to you. Though the Holy Spirit is the free gift of the Father, He is not released without a longing from the aspirant (Isaiah 44:3). You cannot access the power of the Holy Spirit without a thirst for it!

Recognise Jesus as the Baptiser

You must also recognise that Jesus Christ is the Baptiser. He is the One who has the capacity to fill everyone who asks in faith with the Holy Spirit. The Bible is very clear on this,

> *I indeed baptize you with water unto repentance: but he that cometh after me is mightier than I, whose shoes I am not worthy to bear: he shall baptize you with the Holy Ghost, and with fire.*
>
> *Matthew 3:11*

Jesus told His disciples that He will send another Comforter. Therefore, you cannot receive the baptism of the Holy Spirit without first accepting Jesus and acknowledging Him as the giver of the Holy Spirit (John 1:33).

Open Your Heart to the Word

God's Word carries God's Spirit within it and when you open your heart to His Word, the Spirit of God comes into you. In Acts 10:44-46, the Bible says that while Peter was still speaking the Word, the Holy Spirit fell on them that heard, such that they all spoke in tongues. As you are reading this book, allow the words to dwell in your heart, ensure a genuine thirst for the Spirit, and you shall be endued. It is written,

> *...The words that I speak unto you, they are spirit, and they are life.*
>
> *John 6:63*

Ask God in Faith

Though the Holy Spirit is God's gift to believers, you cannot receive Him without asking in faith, because without faith, it is impossible to receive anything from God (James 1:6-7).

Remember: God will not withhold anything good from you. Since the Holy Spirit is God's good gift to you, He will surely grant the desires of your heart (Luke 11:13).

Expect to be Endued with the Holy Spirit

In the Kingdom of God, you are not permitted to receive what you don't expect. Your expectation is what creates the platform for your experience! Therefore, as you desire to be filled with the power of the Holy Spirit, after you have asked the Father for it, you must expect to be filled instantly. The Bible says,

> *For surely there is an end; and thine expectation shall not be cut off.*
>
> *Proverbs 23:18*

Therefore, today, be endued with the power of the Holy Spirit afresh right now, in the name of Jesus!

Open Your Mouth

> *...Open thy mouth wide, and I will fill it.*
>
> *Psalm 81:10*

Having met the above requirements, you must speak with boldness whatever utterance He gives you, believing that He will instantly fill you with His Spirit. It is your bold speaking that shows that you believe Him and that is when the Spirit comes upon you. After He fills you with the power of the Holy Spirit, you must learn to build yourself in this power by constantly speaking in tongues. To grow, you should exercise yourself through your relationship with Him.

This is a personal, non-transferrable responsibility, as no one can be filled, refilled or endowed on your behalf (Acts 4:31).

As you know, every relationship grows well on good and constant communication. This is why you need to effectively and constantly communicate in the language of the Spirit for deeper fellowship, guidance, help and strength.

To relate effectively with the Holy Spirit, among other things, you need to:

Acknowledge His Person

This means to believe in Him, everything He represents and recognise His power, and supremacy over all. The Holy Spirit is the Spirit of God; therefore, He is God Himself. He is neither inferior, nor the least of the Godhead personalities. You must recognise Him as a guide sent to help you. As it is written,

> *But as many as received him, to them gave he power to become the sons of God, even to them that believe on his name:*
>
> John 1:12

If you do not acknowledge the worth of a person, you may not receive much from that person. Even Jesus could not do much in Galilee because the people did not receive Him as a Prophet sent to them (Matthew 13:54-58).

So, to access the power of the Holy Spirit and grow in this power, you must acknowledge His Person and believe that He is able to guide you and make your life comfortable.

Seek His Counsel

One of the major ministries of the Holy Spirit is to guide or counsel you in all areas or issues of life. 'To guide' also means to counsel and when you seek His counsel, you are asking Him for clarity.

Seeking counsel does not necessarily mean you are lost or confused; it just means that you do not want to take a wrong step and as such, you have to involve a higher authority. We all need counsel at one point or the other, and what better counsellor can you involve if not the Holy Spirit? The Word of God says,

> *I will instruct thee and teach thee in the way which thou shalt go: I will guide thee with mine eye.*
> *Psalm 32:8*

One way you can engage Him in counsel is through a prayer of inquiry. For example, you may ask, 'Holy Spirit, which way should I go? Should I do this or should I not?' David, a man after God's heart, engaged this prayer of inquiry when confronted with the challenge of rescuing his people from the Philistines. He asked the Lord,

> *...Shall I pursue after this troop? shall I overtake them? And he answered him, Pursue: for thou shalt surely overtake them, and without fail recover all.*
> *1 Samuel 30:8*

The Holy Spirit is willing to give an answer to every

sincere question you ask, but you must learn to commit your ways to Him. It is written,

> **Trust in the Lord with all thine heart; and lean not unto thine own understanding.**
>
> **In all thy ways acknowledge him, and he shall direct thy paths.**
>
> *Proverbs 3:5-6*

Come to God in Worship

You cannot access the power of the Holy Spirit without first coming to God in worship. 'To worship' means to show or have a strong feeling of admiration or adoration for Him. He deserves your adoration not just because of what He stands to do for you, but because of Who He is. It is written,

> **God is a Spirit: and they that worship him must worship him in spirit and in truth.**
>
> *John 4:24*

Therefore, to relate well with the Holy Spirit, you must learn to reverence God and give Him the honour He deserves.

Be Sensitive to His Voice

The Holy Spirit speaks (1 Timothy 4:1; Hebrews 3:7), but the problem with most believers is that we are not alert to listen to Him. Many people's minds are too occupied with various everyday happenings. To hear the Spirit speak, you need to be sensitive to pick His voice. The Bible says,

Be still, and know that I am God...

Psalm 46:10

Sensitivity means your mind must be calm and void of nuisance. It also means that your heart must be right without offence. As it is written,

I was in the Spirit on the Lord's day, and heard behind me a great voice, as of a trumpet.

Revelation 1:10

Remember: The Holy Spirit has a still small voice (1 Kings 19:12), and to hear a small voice requires your alertness. Therefore, sensitivity is a must.

Having known how to relate with the Holy Spirit, you must also learn to enjoy His leading continuously. For you to be constantly led by the Holy Spirit, consider the following:

Be Spiritual: Being born again is very different from being spiritual, because it is possible to be born again and not be spiritual. However, you cannot be spiritual and not be born again. Spirituality is not religion or going to church, it is living your life in line with God's Word. Scripture says,

For to be carnally minded is death; but to be

spiritually minded is life and peace.

Romans 8:6

The truth is: The Holy Spirit will not lead a carnal man, because he cannot have access to Him, neither can he understand what the Spirit says. The Word of God says,

> **And the spirit entered into me when he spake unto me, and set me upon my feet, that I heard him that spake unto me.**
>
>
>
> *Ezekiel 2:2*
>
>

Be Humble: For you to be led by the Holy Spirit, humility is very vital. Proud people are too full of themselves; they never accept that they do not know, neither do they acknowledge their faults. At times, when you consider the leading of the Holy Spirit with human instincts, it may seem unrealistic or too simple to be the solution, but you have to accept that He knows all things and He is always right. It is written,

> **The meek will he guide in judgment: and the meek will he teach his way.**
>
>
>
> *Psalm 25:9*
>
>

This is why the proud cannot be led by Him. Humility entails acknowledging the Holy Spirit as the Doer and not taking the glory for it. Also, you must be able to accept when He reveals your wrongs to you. When all these are in place, you are sure to enjoy an unhindered flow of His leadings and revelations.

Be Still: To be led by the Spirit, you must learn to be quiet in your spirit. This quietness has nothing to do with physical disposition, but your mind being peaceful. The Bible enjoins us to study to be quiet (1 Thessalonians 4:11).

You do not need to be in prayer or in the church before the Holy Spirit can speak to you. He speaks everywhere, even in places as busy as the market, but it takes the stillness of your spirit-man to pick what He says, when He says it. Scripture says,

> *Be still, and know that I am God: I will be exalted among the heathen, I will be exalted in the earth.*
>
> *Psalm 46:10*

Be Joyful: This is one of the cheapest ways to access the leading of the Holy Spirit. Joy is an attractor; it brings great things into one's life. More so, it creates an avenue for the Holy Spirit to dwell because He cannot survive in a sad environment. He is the Spirit of joy; whatever wants to break your joy wants to rob you of access to His power. When you are sad, you keep the Holy Spirit away from you. As it is written,

> *Therefore with joy shall ye draw water out of the wells of salvation.*
>
> *Isaiah 12:3*

Right now, I curse the spirit of sadness off your life and destiny, in Jesus name!

However, it is not enough to be empowered with the Holy Spirit, we must also grow in Him. Growth is a continuous process and as such requires your constant engagement or exercise, spiritually and otherwise. It is written,

> **Quench not the Spirit.**
>
> *1 Thessalonians 5:19*

Just as a body without proper food and nutrition will be stunted and can die, the Holy Spirit in you, without being properly nourished, can be quenched or caused to be non-functional.

Remember: To dominate in this wicked world, you need an ever-increasing enduement of power. The Bible says,

> **Wherefore I put thee in remembrance that thou stir up the gift of God...**
>
> *2 Timothy 1:6*

To stir up the gift of the Holy Spirit in you, therefore, you should engage daily in the following, among other things:

Praying Always in the Spirit: Praying in the Spirit is a spiritual exercise designed to build and strengthen your spirit-man. When you pray in the Spirit, which is speaking in an unknown tongue, your spirit is praying and that makes you speak outside the realm of the flesh. It is written,

But ye, beloved, building up yourselves on your
most holy faith, praying in the Holy Ghost,

Jude 20

The flesh is usually selfish and most of the time, not in accordance with God's will. When you pray in the Spirit, you cannot pray amiss and the devil cannot understand you because you are speaking mysteries to God. This grants you unhindered answers to prayers (Roman 8:27).

I have discovered that the more you pray in the Spirit, the stronger and more effective your prayer life becomes, thereby empowering you to become a terror to the enemy. It is wisdom to engage in this regularly as the Spirit leads. You do not have to be in church or a secluded place to pray in the Spirit. Remember that you are to pray without ceasing (1 Thessalonians 5:17).

Learn to Listen: The Holy Spirit speaks only to those who will listen to what He has to say. Listening does not only mean hearing or being able to pick signals; it also means adhering to His instructions, corrections and reproofs as He gives you per time. Scripture says,

God hath spoken once; twice have I heard this; that
power belongeth unto God.

Psalm 62:11

Walking with the Holy Spirit requires that you understand Him, and you cannot understand Him if you do not submit to Him by obeying Him.

For instance, if you have a friend who always runs to you for advice but never applies it, you will at a point stop giving advice to that person; so it is with the Holy Spirit. You will never be left alone, in the name of Jesus!

Constant Word Study: Daily study of the Word of God is one way to build yourself in the Spirit, because the Word is Spirit-based and is the inspiration of the Holy Spirit. So, He speaks constantly by the Word. When you exercise yourself in the Word, you are building yourself spiritually to be led by the Spirit. As it is written,

> *It is the spirit that quickeneth; the flesh profiteth nothing: the words that I speak unto you, they are spirit, and they are life.*
>
> John 6:63

God's Word builds, fortifies, sanctifies and increases your barns. It builds you by developing your faith and trust in God. It also sanctifies you and makes you fit for the indwelling of the Spirit.

The Word also builds your ability to hear the Holy Spirit. When you study the Word of God regularly, it grows your ability to hear the Spirit and the deeper you go in the Word, the clearer His voice to you. So, as you study the Word of God, watch out for the voice of the Holy Spirit and He will surely speak to you. George Muller said: 'If the Holy Spirit guides us, He will do it according to the scriptures and never contrary to them'.

Prayer and Fasting

The period of prayer and fasting is a period of renewal of strength. It does not just mean staying away from food, but setting out time to gain spiritual energy by engaging the Word, studying anointed books and praying effectively. This is a very effective way to build yourself in the Holy Spirit. It is written,

> **But they that wait upon the LORD shall renew their strength; they shall mount up with wings as eagles; they shall run, and not be weary; and they shall walk, and not faint.**
>
> *Isaiah 40:31*

Fasting is prescribed for the empowerment, re-empowerment and continuous empowerment of the saints because it is meant to break every yoke that may want to stand against your spiritual growth (Isaiah 58:6). So, you must engage practically in fasting as a programme in your life.

Please beware: Fasting is not meant to be an emergency weapon but a life-long programme for every believer. It is not a thing you do once in a while; it should be scheduled because it is designed for your continuous and sustainable relevance.

My prayer is that you will never lose touch with the power from on high, in Jesus name!

'Men ought to seek with their whole hearts to be filled with the Spirit of God. Without being filled with the Spirit, it is utterly impossible that an individual Christian or a church can ever live or work as God desires'

- Andrew Murray

Conclusion

As I conclude this book, let me sound a note of caution here. The Holy Spirit is a person and therefore, can be grieved. To 'grieve' Him means to cause Him to be angry and this can quench or cause Him to withdraw from you. The Bible says,

> **And grieve not the Holy Spirit of God, whereby ye are sealed unto the day of redemption.**
>
> *Ephesians 4:30*

One way you can grieve Him is to wilfully engage in sin, after you have known the truth as revealed by the Word of God. You must be very careful to listen to His voice and respond when He cautions.

Some consequences of grieving the Spirit include, but are not limited to:

- Loss of the assurance of salvation (Romans 8:16)

- Loss of interest in studying the Bible (Mark 4:11)

- Absence of the fruits of the Spirit in your life (John 6:63)

- Compromise of your ability to tell right from wrong (2 Corinthians 11:3)

- Loss of your faith in God and His works (John 12:40)

- Feeling of hopelessness when confronted with even the minutest challenge (Job 8:13-14).

From the depth of my heart, I pray that you shall neither grieve the Holy Spirit nor quench Him. Right now, receive a fresh release of the power of the Holy Spirit upon your life in a growing dimension that will distinguish you on the earth and secure your place in eternity, in Jesus name!

The Salvation Prayer

The only condition God requires of you to become His child is to accept Jesus Christ as your Lord and personal Saviour (Romans 10:10). Having considered this truth, you can now say this prayer:

Father, I realise that I have been a sinner.

Today, I come before You asking for forgiveness of my sins.

I believe in the death and resurrection of Jesus Christ and I believe in His power to save me if I ask Him to.

Now Lord, save me, accept me as Your child and write my name in the Book of Life.

Thank you Father for saving me in Jesus name.

I receive and accept You today as my Lord and personal Saviour.

Amen.

Holy Ghost Baptism Prayer

You have read this book, understood its content and desire to be endued with the power of the Holy Spirit; then, you have made the wisest choice ever! The truth is: You cannot survive this world without the Holy Spirit dwelling and working through you.

If you desire to be baptised in the Holy Ghost and be endued with His power, you can ask Him right now by praying this prayer with faith from the depth of your heart:

> *Dear God,*
> *I desire the baptism of the Holy Spirit.*
> *Your Word says if I ask, I will receive the Holy Spirit.*
> *I believe with all my heart that Your Word is true.*
> *Therefore, I ask that You fill me to overflowing with Your precious Holy Spirit, in the name of Jesus Christ.*
> *I also believe that Jesus is the Baptiser, as I was told.*
> *Therefore, baptise me in the Holy Spirit, now.*
> *Thank You Jesus, for by faith, I receive and believe that I now have the Holy Spirit right inside me.*
> *Holy Spirit, I fully expect to speak with other tongues, as You give me the utterance, in Jesus name I pray.*
> *Amen!*

Now, open your mouth and begin to pray aloud, allowing the Holy Spirit to pray through you in other tongues.

Congratulations!